THE UNITED NATIONS AND THE WORLD'S RELIGIONS: PROSPECTS FOR A GLOBAL ETHIC

• • •

*Proceedings of a Conference held
October 7, 1994, at Columbia University*

Cosponsored by
School of International and Public Affairs
and the Department of Religion
Columbia University
and
Boston Research Center for the 21st Century
in collaboration with
International Mahavir Jain Mission
and
Soka Gakkai International

Organized by
Southern Asian Institute
Columbia University

Published by
Boston Research Center for the 21st Century
396 Harvard Street
Cambridge, MA 02138-3924

Library of Congress catalogue card number: 95-80161
ISBN 1-887917-00-4

Edited by Nancy Hodes and Michael Hays
Layout/design by Ralph Buglass
Cover design by Susan Brennan
Conference photographs by Jonathan Wilson

TABLE OF CONTENTS

• • •

PREFACE

• • •

The invitation to this conference sent out by Columbia University's Southern Asian Institute included two hope-filled observations—one by a diplomat and the other by a theologian:

> *It is possible to discern an increasingly common moral perception that spans the world's nations and peoples, and which is finding expression in international laws, many owing their genesis to the work of this organization.*
>
> —UN Secretary-General
> Boutros Boutros-Ghali,
> *An Agenda for Peace* (1992)

> *Perhaps one day there may even be a United Nations Declaration on a Global Ethic to provide moral support for the Declaration on Human Rights, which is so often ignored and cruelly violated.*
>
> —Hans Küng,
> Preface to *A Global Ethic* (1993)

Together, these two quotations frame both the context and the aspirations that led the cosponsoring organizations to convene what Robert Thurman has called a "bold adventure of the imagination," an adventure in which you, the reader, are about to take part.

As you share in our discussion, we hope the full measure of the ardor, energy and sense of expectation that marked this fascinating day come through to you. The editors, Michael Hays and Nancy Hodes, have taken pains to preserve the flavor not only of what was said but of the sincerity and directness of the speakers as they engaged in sometimes difficult exchanges. On behalf of the cosponsors and participating speakers, we at the Boston Research Center for the 21st Century are proud to offer you what we feel is a truly inspiring and yet down-to-earth set of dialogues on the Human Rights Declaration and the Global Ethic.

In addition to the plenary event, please don't overlook the appendix which reproduces the highlights of the group discussions. They illustrate the continuing validity of Dr. Samuel Johnson's time-honored perception about values. As Sissela Bok reminds us in these pages, he understood that values, in order to be meaningful, need to be "put to the use of life."

So do good books. We will consider this book one if it finds its way into the hearts of even a few of the decent people everywhere who are struggling to exemplify and encourage humane values in an increasingly violent, trouble-filled world.

FOREWORD

. . .

Reading the transcript of this conference, I was delighted to return in mind to that pleasant and stimulating day in the Kellogg Center, atop the International Affairs Building at Columbia. I am pleased to think that many readers can participate with us in our bold adventure of the imagination. Envision a world where all the religions really do collaborate to support a United Nations that effectively maintains a humane ethic for a world society! I write again here to bring out a few essential further points.

It is inspiring to contemplate the coming into being of a civilized world society. Looking back at our title, I think one word could have been added, the word "humane"—"Prospects for a Humane Global Ethic." By adding that word, the task seems more plausible if only by virtue of the patent impossibility of not undertaking it!

That is to say, we do now have a global ethic. It is an ethic too strongly tilted toward the worship of power, the rule of brute force, the culture of violence. It is an ethic based on the assumption that there is no reliable civilization. Civility—humane, altruistically tinged treatment of persons by each other due to a shared perception of commonality between them—may prevail occasionally within specific membership groups, some families, some communities, some times. But it is unrealistic to expect a code of civility to prevail worldwide. Given acceptance of a status quo dictated by an underlying presence of ruthless power, there can be a show of civility on the surface. But the reality of things is an order maintained by violence, always threatened and frequently manifest.

So there is no problem about achieving a global ethic. It is not an unrealistic task. We have a global ethic. The problem is that it is all too clearly an uncivilized ethic. It is a surface texture of ordered interaction, thinly stretched over the bottomless abyss of the relentless violence of the all-out struggle for ultimate power.

The key of civility, everyone will grant, lies in all inter-actors sharing a commonality of identity, a sense of kinship and mutuality of interests. Family familiarity, tribal membership, national affiliation, racial affinity, and religious community—these all have shown themselves capable of anchoring such a commonality of identity in groups of people. This sense of common identity enables them, occasionally and temporarily, to overcome the root egocentrism that makes all human relationships unstable and unreliable, even the most intimate. The problem then is how to create a global commonality of identity that could anchor a deeply internalized sense of world community. When the majority of humans feel a sense of common "earthi-ness," they will naturally wish to act within the forms of a true civility with other Earthans, will naturally strive to treat each other in altruistically tinged—that is *kindly*—ways. There is the emergence of a reliably humane global ethic.

Secular nationalism has been able to transcend differences of tribe and race at times, but not reliably, as we can see from the failure of the last three supernationalisms, Soviet, Chinese, and, I am afraid, even American, to provide the effective sense of a national identity beyond ethnic, class, race, and gender identity. These supernationalisms seemed stable for a while by adding ideological identity—communist or democratic—to national identity, and engaging in extensive propaganda, thought reform, and repression. The unraveling of the USSR, the near-unraveling, broad disaffection within the PRC, and the seemingly inexorable shredding of the delicate tissues of civility by intensifying class, race, and even gender polarization within the USA are making clear at the moment the instability of identity provided by nationalisms and supernationalisms.

The world religions, on the other hand—the most anciently universalistic of them, Buddhism, Jainism, Christianity, and Islam, along with various modern universalist movements, such as Sikhism, Baha'ism, and others—have demonstrated over centuries that they are capable of providing a source of common identity that can occasionally and at least partially transcend differences of clan, tribe, nation, and even race (gender difference transcendence is a theoretical possibility for these movements but rarely up to now an actuality). There-fore, they may hold the key to the identity expansion that is required to undergird a new global civility. That key is a sense of *spiritual* mem-bership, transcendent identity with an infinite life force, conceived of as either a Creator God or a Truth Presence Enlightened Being. This seems to be the deepest level of identity-sense, capable of transcend-ing tribal, racial, and gender identities, and creating a durable sense of community within which a humane ethic can flourish.

However, even these religious universalisms have so far exhibited one limiting factor. They have proven overall incapable of expanding their sense of identity to include those outside their faiths. The Bud-dhists are the most inclusive, due to their distinctive teaching of self-lessness and emptiness of everything, including the Truth Presence of Infinite Compassion. But even Buddhists feel that the others will have to become Buddhists eventually in order to become enlightened and free of suffering. The Muslims do include Christianity, as their own nearest precursor in worship of the same God, while their attitude to-ward Buddhists as nonbelievers has been hostile through history. The Christians love the same God as the Muslims, but have been intolerant of the Muslim refusal to accept the Unique Saviorship of Christ, while they continue to be hard on the Buddhists and Jains due to their per-sistent nonbelief. The more modern universalisms have the widest theo-retical tolerance, though they are also uncomfortable with the "nontheism" or "infinitheism" of the Buddhists.

His Holiness the Dalai Lama has often stated his personal belief that it is time for the world religions to make whatever changes are necessary to abandon competition with one another. I was delighted to find that Daisaku Ikeda has called for different religions to turn their competitiveness away from exclusivity and rather towards the task of producing good world citizens. Visionaries in other traditions have also made the same appeal. To date, however, none of the world reli-gions as a whole has yet come up with a call for a full mutual interinclusion by world religions of each others' members—*even in the all-important ethical sense*. Quite the contrary. Each wants to include all the others only by converting those others' members to its vision of the world. This tendency makes for mutual intolerance, and will inevita-bly lead to violence in the future as it has done so often in the past.

On the side of secularism, the modern Human Rights tradition dignifies secularism itself as an effective world religion by providing it *in theory* with a framework of ethical principles that should restrain individuals' and states' mistreatment of other individuals. Human rights thinkers in general have considered religions as obstacles to worldwide acceptance of their humane principles, and always call attention to the religions' intolerance of nonbelievers and outsiders. But the industrial nations wherein the Human Rights traditions have developed have themselves not yet been able to live up to the strong standards called for by Human Rights declarations. They have subjected and continue to subject outsiders to atrocious mistreatment and exploitation, and they have not sufficiently extended the network of compassion and civility to the weaker members of their own societies. If they can confront their own record with a critical clear-sightedness, they will perhaps make a stronger effort to discover how much the world religions have accomplished through their long histories in assisting huge and diverse populations to develop better manners of treating each other more humanely, within a sense of common brotherhood and sisterhood, being children of God or being potential Buddhas, protégés of the infinite Enlightened Beings throughout the universe.

In such a spirit, it should be possible for the leaders and members of the world religions to join with the enlightened secularists of the Human Rights tradition to develop realistic "minimalist" (in the insightful formulation of Sissela Bok) standards of humane ethical behavior, and then, as importantly, use the far-flung networks of world religious institutions—adding the temples, mosques, and churches to the "universal ethical internet," so to speak—to educate their flocks gradually to implement these ethical principles in interactions, to secure the human rights of all people on this earth.

Recently a friend of mine gave me a copy of the following quotation from Goethe, which gives real heart to our audacious enterprise:

> *Until one is committed there is always hesitancy, the chance to draw back, always ineffectiveness. Concerning all acts of initiative and creation, there is one elementary truth, the ignorance of which kills countless ideas and splendid plans: the moment one definitely commits oneself, then Providence moves too. All sorts of things occur to help that would never have occurred. A whole stream of events issues from the decision, raising to one's favor all manner of unforeseen accidents and meetings and material assistance which no man*

could have dreamed would come his way. Whatever you can do or dream you can, begin it. Boldness has genius, power and magic in it.

— **Robert A.F. Thurman**
Professor of Indo-Tibetan
Buddhism and Chairperson
of the Department of Religion
Columbia University

PROGRAM OF THE DAY

• • •

Welcoming Remarks
Virginia Straus, Boston Research Center for the 21st Century

Opening Remarks
Robert A.F. Thurman, Department of Religion, Columbia University

Panel #1 - The Universal Declaration of Human Rights
Louis Henkin, School of Law, Columbia University
Richard Falk, Center for International Studies, Princeton University

Panel #2 - Perspectives on a Global Ethic and Common Values
Mark Juergensmeyer (moderator), Department of Sociology, University of California, Santa Barbara
Sissela Bok, Harvard Center for Population and Development Studies
Robert A.F. Thurman, Department of Religion, Columbia University

Open Discussion

Panel #3 - The World's Religions: Prospects for a Global Ethic in Support of Human Rights
Fr. Luis Dolan (moderator), UN Representative, Temple of Understanding
Peter Awn, Department of Religion, Columbia University
Rebequa Getahoun Murphy, UN Representative, Baha'is of the US
Sallie B. King, Department of Philosophy and Religion, James Madison University

Open Discussion

Small Group Discussions

Plenary Session - Reports from group discussions
   Mark Juergensmeyer (moderator), Department of Sociology, University of California, Santa Barbara

Concluding Remarks
   Harvey Cox, Harvard Divinity School, Harvard University

Closing
   Robert A.F. Thurman, Department of Religion, Columbia University

Reception

Music at the conference was provided by
Symphony for the United Nations
under the direction of Maestro Joseph Eger

Plenary session in Kellogg Center.

Jonathan Wilson

Open discussion at the Plenary.

The presentations offered new insights for young scholars.

The United Nations and the World's Religions:
Prospects for a Global Ethic

• • •

CONFERENCE PROCEEDINGS

WELCOMING REMARKS

• • •

By Virginia Straus

Virginia Straus is Executive Director of the Boston Research Center for the 21st Century. She is a public policy specialist who formerly directed the Pioneer Institute, a state and local policy think tank in Boston, which she helped to establish in 1987. She worked for nine years in Washington, D.C., serving first as a legislative researcher in the House of Representatives and as a financial analyst in the Treasury Department and then later as an urban policy aide in the Carter White House.

Welcome, and good morning! I'm happy to see so many people here today, and pleased that this conference has generated more interest than we could reasonably have expected.

What we hope to come out with at the end of today is a holistic view of two related conversations that sometimes take place quite separately—the dialogue among international affairs specialists about the Universal Declaration of Human Rights, and the dialogue among religionists about the global ethic. For this purpose, we are happy to be bringing together such diversity. We have in this room people of different religions and beliefs. We have the Religion Department joining with the School of International and Public Affairs—not a

> **"By not only accepting or merely tolerating these differences, but actually enjoying them, according to Buddhist thought, we realize our connectedness with each other at a deeper level, and ultimately create harmony of a lasting nature."**

common sight at most universities. We have scholars along with activists, and I'm sure many other differences among us.

By not only accepting or merely tolerating these differences, but actually enjoying them, according to Buddhist thought, we realize our connectedness with each other at a deeper level, and ultimately create harmony of a lasting nature.

It seems most appropriate that the Southern Asian Institute, devoted to the study of such a culturally diverse region of the world, would be our host today. I want in particular to thank and recognize Barbara Gombach for coordinating this conference. She put in months of cheerful, good-humored, persistent, and professional effort. She was ably assisted by Bob Cessna and a busy cadre of students.

I would also like to express my appreciation to the Institute's director, Jack Hawley, who by a quirk of fate had to be at another conference today, to International Affairs Dean Robin Lewis, Professor Robert Thurman, President George Rupp, and Professor Harvey Cox for the crucial early support they gave us in developing the idea for this conference.

The Boston Research Center for the 21st Century is devoted to peace research, but not in the usual sense of research as a solitary activity. Our emphasis is on dialogue, the pooling of wisdom. We support conferences at various US universities and conversations at the Center among small but diverse groups of scholars on peace-related issues such as nonviolence, human rights, and UN reform.

In this mission, we follow in the footsteps of the Center's founder, Daisaku Ikeda, who is president of the Soka Gakkai International and for decades has conducted exchanges of Eastern and Western views for the sake of peace on many subjects with scholars and activists around the world. He spoke about the role of religion at a lecture he gave a year ago at Harvard University called "Mahayana Buddhism and 21st Century Civilization." He said it is not specific religions but the religious sensibility, or, as John Dewey called it, simply "the religious" that is important. He said, "It is only through fusing with the eternal—that which lies beyond our finitude as individuals—that we can manifest the full scale of our potential." This "fusing with the eternal" is the outgrowth of dialogue at its best.

Today's conference is especially meaningful in the Center's history because it marks the one-year anniversary of our founding. So, in addition to celebrating differences today, we celebrate our birthday with you. We will now enjoy a brief presentation by the Symphony for the United Nations, providing what I am sure will be an experience in musical harmony that will linger in our minds during the day's discussion.

OPENING REMARKS

• • •

By Robert A.F. Thurman

Robert A.F. Thurman is Jey Tsong Khapa Pro-
fessor on Indo-Tibetan Buddhism at Columbia
University and Chairperson of the Department
of Religion. After receiving his PhD in Sanskrit
and Indian Studies from Harvard University in
1972, he taught at Amherst College and Boston
University. Professor Thurman is a founding
trustee of the American Institute of Buddhist
Studies.

Welcome, everybody. The room is almost full, which is amazing, and wonderful. As I was listening to that beautiful music that we just had the privilege of hearing, I was thinking that academic conferences usually don't have such an introduction. You never get a chance to remember the harmony of the universe before you get into whatever it is you're going to quarrel about. (*laughter*) So this really is a much better way to start, and I think it's of benefit to bring this kind of consideration to bear on the reality of the world today with its dire situation.

The second thing the music made me think, that impossibly beautiful music of Mozart, is that many people in this city and in this world would consider the very topic of our conference as in fact

"I think that the spirit we must bring to the conference...is the spirit not to allow our preconceptions and our conditioning as to what is possible and what is realistic to suppress our insistence that the good and the intelligent shall prevail over the mad and the nasty."

7

preposterous. They would consider us hopeless idealists to be hoping that some miraculous thing will happen, given a situation where there are a lot of hard realities that make any kind of positive outcome, or the notion of a global ethic, completely impossible to realize. Please don't consider me a pessimist in acknowledging that, however, and please don't go home right now.

I think that the spirit we must bring to the conference today, inspired by the Boston Research Center for the 21st Century that has sponsored our gathering, is the only spirit in which we're going to reach the 21st century. It is the spirit not to allow our preconceptions and our conditioning as to what is possible and what is realistic to suppress our insistence that the good and the intelligent shall prevail over the mad and the nasty. Ever since I was a little child, whenever anything good would happen, I would always think just before it happened that something would disturb it, and it would not come to be after all. Even a birthday party, for example: I would think that something would go wrong and the cake wouldn't arrive. I have since realized that I'm conditioned that way, and perhaps many of us are. So it's wonderful to be at a conference where we're bluntly and blithely going ahead into an area of hope and prayer and careful thought, into how to develop some sort of principle, some sort of inspiration for a sensible and sane way to move into the future instead of the way in which we have been going, which clearly is not going to get us to the future.

Panel #1

• • •

THE UNIVERSAL DECLARATION OF HUMAN RIGHTS: THE FRAMERS AND THEIR VISIONS

• • •

Louis Henkin
School of Law, Columbia University

Richard Falk
Center for International Studies, Princeton University

Panel #1 Presentation by

LOUIS HENKIN

• • •

Louis Henkin is University Professor Emeritus at Columbia University. He is the author of numerous books and articles on law and foreign affairs. Professor Henkin is a Fellow of the American Academy of Arts and Sciences, and a member of the American Philosophical Society, and of the Institute of International Law.

I am pleased to be here, and to talk to you about religion and the Universal Declaration of Human Rights.

The relationship between religion and human rights is not very clear and not well understood. Perhaps, as Ms. Straus suggested, there has been no relationship, or little relationship, between the two. They have existed in two different universes. Ideas about religion and ideas about human rights, and the people involved in the two fields of thought and inquiry, have not had frequent points of meeting. This conference, and other recent developments—including a program now underway at Columbia—reflect an effort to bring religion and human rights into some harmony, at least into some awareness of each other.

The reasons for the dissociation of human rights and religion are historical, political, and intellectual. Contrary to some impressions (and some self-serving claims), organized religions have

"We have to accept the Universal Declaration as the basis for a global ethic, perhaps polished and adjusted to take accout of the ambiguities injected by the Cold War. But one ought to recognize that the Universal Declaration and human rights are not, and were not intended to be, a complete global ethic."

not been principal contributors to the idea of human rights. Students of religion or of the history of religion will agree, I believe, that though natural law has authentic religious roots or links, the idea of natural rights does not. The religions that I know something about are not religions of rights, but of duties, of commandments. When the Bible commands me to "love thy neighbor as thyself," I have a duty to love my neighbor, but we do not think of the neighbor as having a right to be loved. In that conception, if anybody has rights, it is God: I have a duty to obey God; He has the right to be obeyed. The neighbor, a lawyer might say, is a third party beneficiary. (*laughter*)

The traditional religions have not emphasized the rights of individuals. What is more, one of the key values in the idea of human rights is individual autonomy; but the older religions, while insisting that the individual has free will, have not valued individual autonomy. Doing what is right in one's own eyes is not a good; in essence, it is anarchy.

If any religion might claim to have contributed to the idea of human rights, it would be Protestant Christianity, which puts emphasis on the individual. From my reading of intellectual history, the first assertion of a universal human right seems to have been by Protestant dissenting bodies, the Levellers in particular, in the 17th century. It was then that we saw the beginnings of the idea of rights as deriving from some superior law—superior to the law of the king and to that of the republics which followed. It was then that rights were seen as individual and, what is more, universal. And those notions underlie the idea of rights as it is reflected in the Universal Declaration of Human Rights.

Having denied the claims of religion to paternity of the idea, I hasten to recognize and affirm that religion has nonetheless made major contributions to human rights. Religion is a source of ethics, and a foundation of morality, the theme of your conference today. Also, the Universal Declaration roots human rights in human dignity, a value not alien to religion. Religions also contributed the conception and the details of justice which are essential to the idea of rights and which permeate every particular provision of the Universal Declaration.

A more difficult question, which I hope you will discuss, is the relevance of religion to the universality of human rights. "Western" religions declare that man was created in the image of God, and that all men and women have a common human ancestor. That suggests the brotherhood of man, which ought to lead to universality. But religion has not always led to brotherhood; in fact, it has often contributed to hostility rather than to love, to dissent rather than to consent, bringing human rights violations such as those that trouble the world today. Then religion earns not credit but blame, not credit for its contribution to human rights but blame for their violation.

Now to the Declaration—and religion.

Freedom of religion is clearly a basic element in the contemporary ideology of rights. A few here will recall, and most of you will have learned, that President Franklin Delano Roosevelt, in 1941, delivered a famous address in which he spoke about Four Freedoms, which became a rallying cry during the Second World War and an agenda for the peace to follow. Roosevelt's Four Freedoms were: freedom of speech, freedom of religion (the link to our discussion), freedom from want (then a very progressive idea), and freedom from fear (by which he meant freedom from invasion by people such as Hitler). Today the Four Freedoms seem dated: Roosevelt was not yet aware of the need to establish freedom from genocide or freedom from torture.

Those who drafted the Universal Declaration doubtless had the Four Freedoms in mind. (Eleanor Roosevelt was chair of the commission that drafted the Universal Declaration.) So it is perhaps surprising that religion did not loom larger, did not figure more prominently, in the Universal Declaration. There is a reference to freedom of belief in the preamble to the Declaration. Article 18 provides that everyone has the right to freedom of thought, conscience, and religion.

Why isn't freedom of religion more prominent? One of the reasons is not difficult to guess. The framers were trying to prepare a declaration acceptable to all, including the "socialist world," i.e., the communist world, to which religion was the "opiate of the people." Among the principal participants in preparing and promulgating the Declaration were representatives of Stalin, who had to be placated and persuaded. The Universal Declaration is a most remarkable instrument, perhaps the most important document of the twentieth century, indeed one of the notable instruments mankind has produced; but it is a product of the beginnings of the Cold War, and it had to take account of essential dissonance between East and West on important matters.

It would be important to scrutinize the Universal Declaration today for signs of ambivalence, of ambiguity, of "papering over" differences, let us say, between Eleanor Roosevelt and Josef Stalin. Recall the vote on the Universal Declaration. At that time there were fewer than sixty participating states (instead of today's one hundred and ninety, or so). Forty-eight of them voted for the Declaration, while eight abstained. Among the abstainers were all the members of the Communist world of the time (China was not yet a Communist country, and Yugoslavia, later ambivalent, was a full member of the bloc). South Africa abstained, for reasons we readily understand. Saudi Arabia, an Islamic country, also abstained, probably for reasons that will have to be addresssed when we discuss why major religions have not been able to agree on a global ethic.

In my view, the Universal Declaration should be recognized by the religious world (and by the non-religious world) as an authentic foundation for a global ethic. The commitment in the Declaration to the human dignity of every human being and to the principles of justice should be acceptable to all. The particular rights recognized in the Declaration should be acceptable to all.

But there is an area of important dissonance, and to a large extent it is rooted in religion. When the Declaration was converted into binding covenants, and states began to append reservations, we found a number of them to be religiously inspired. We in the United States tend lightly to assume that all—surely all religions—should be pleased in particular with Article 18 of the Universal Declaration: the right to freedom of thought, conscience, and religion. In fact, some religions do not accept freedom of religion for others. Article 18 also declares that this right includes freedom to change one's religion or belief, and the freedom "either alone or in community with others, and in public or in private, to manifest [that] religion or belief." The freedom to change one's religion or belief, and the right of some others to manifest their religion, are not acceptable to a number of religions.

Religious dissent from the human rights ideology concentrates on yet another basic principle; the religions of the world are not all committed to gender equality. This is not the place to debate the issue of separate (but equal) spheres, of "the public and the private," but gender equality has been a principal focus of reservations to the principal conventions and to the Convention on Discrimination against Women. (I like the full title of that convention: "Convention on the Elimination of all Forms of Discrimination against Women," modeled on the "Convention on the Elimination of all Forms of Racial Discrimination.") The religious world must face the demand of gender equality.

Respect for the religion of others and respect for women, then, are two themes which I commend to you as problems to be faced in trying to develop a global ethic.

A final point. We have to accept the Universal Declaration as the basis for a global ethic, perhaps polished and adjusted to take account of the ambiguities injected by the Cold War. But one ought to recognize that the Universal Declaration and human rights are not, and were not intended to be, a complete global ethic. It is a minimal ethic. Rights, human rights, are essential, but not enough. The Declaration, the ideology of rights, say nothing about brotherhood, or love, or friendship, or other goods and other values that should be the concern of religion. But we won't have any of them unless we start with this particular foundation, a foundation of rights.

I commend to you the Universal Declaration as the essence of a global ethic. To that end, picking up the theme that Ms. Straus launched for us, there is a need for institutions in the world of religion and institutions in the world of human rights to talk to each other and to help each other in that common cause—to establish rights as the basis of a universal ethic.

RICHARD FALK

• • •

Richard A. Falk, Albert G. Milbank Professor of International Law and Practice at Princeton University, has devoted himself to the analysis of the political relations among peoples and nations. He received his L.L.B. from Yale Law School and Doctorate of Jurisprudence from Harvard University. Professor Falk has written and edited numerous books. His most recent are Revitalizing International Law *and* Explorations at the Edge of Time: Prospects for World Order.

I must say that it's only slightly less intimidating to follow Lou Henkin to the podium than for a composer to play his piece after the audience has listened to Mozart—especially on this subject. But it's a great privilege to be part of this conference, and I feel very committed to my understanding of what it is seeking to achieve. I want to reinforce one of the themes addressed by Professor Henkin, namely, that the Universal Declaration is a remarkable document. This is particularly true given the period in which it was drafted and agreed upon by states that—as he suggested through his reference to the Cold War—had already realized how fundamental their differences were about the ways in which society and human affairs should be organized.

I would also stress that the Declaration was very much the product of a secular humanist sensibility. Indeed, I believe the place of religion was deliberately kept at the margins of its statements

"What we need at this stage if we are to create a universally viable global ethic is to focus on economic and social rights as deserving priority and serious attention. Unless this happens it will always seem to most of the peoples of the world that human rights are little more than a luxury of the affluent."

on human rights. This was done in part to protect the right of religion and the practice of religion from any implication of political control, but religion in general was also subsumed under a wider humanist ethos, one derived primarily from the Enlightenment and the emergence of a liberal-democratic, scientific civilization that placed its hopes for human progress on the material capacities of society, whether Marxist or capitalist. Of course, these two ideological systems had different images of how human dignity was to be achieved, but they shared an underlying secularism and, in a sense, an underlying materialism as the foundation for their conceptions of a global ethic, although the Marxist-Leninist tradition was explicitly hostile to religion while liberalism celebrated its role within private space.

I want to add, though, that in addition to describing the achievements of this document, it is also important to discuss its limitations. And, in my view, these limitations can best be understood in terms of four main categories of difficulties, all of which are related to the fact that the Universal Declaration is incomplete as a text. As Lou said, it's a minimum ethic. But in establishing this minimum, the Declaration remained normatively blind to certain issues that have since become crucial to the development of an adequate global ethic. It was normatively blind, for instance, to the distinctive circumstances of indigenous peoples. And for that reason indigenous peoples have been working with surprising success to evolve their own universal declaration—a parallel declaration of the rights of indigenous peoples. This appears necessary because, to a very important degree, the Universal Declaration is a humanist ethic of modern civilization. Thus, however one might want to characterize the diverse world views of indigenous peoples, whether pre-modern, non-modern, or whatever, they were not part of the sensibilities that inspired and informed the Universal Declaration.

Broadly speaking, group rights were very much ignored, including the right of self-determination, which has, in a sense, become the right of rights. Even though the UN Charter mentions self-determination, within the specific framework of human rights, self-determination was not mentioned until the covenants were agreed upon in 1966. This issue is extremely important because it relates to the problem of captive peoples and nations. In other words, the notion of self-determination must be applied not only in the anti-colonial context, but in relation to the problems of the Kurdish peoples and the Tibetan people, and it must also address the needs of peoples that are "nations" but have been enclosed within statist interpretations of political identity and, thus, defined in ways that do not correspond to the existential reality of these peoples themselves. A denial of self-determination in such settings leads not to the protection, but to the annihilation of their essential identity. I think the Kurdish and Tibetan cases are extremely vivid in suggesting the degree to which self-determination, if tied exclusively to the state, is oppressive to ethnic groups and autonomous peoples caught within its ethnically artificial boundaries. We understood this in a kind of Cold War sense in relation to Eastern Europe, but there the problems of statehood and nationhood were not yet clearly disjoined. However, the events in Yugoslavia suggest how pathologically disconnected they can become if the process of dissolution is not handled in a more successful manner.

The second area of incompleteness is also one that Professor Henkin alluded to, but I would like to take it a little further. If I understood him correctly, he emphasized gender equality, but I think there is really more involved here, including the realms of sexual identity and reproductive rights. In a way that is analogous to problems of indigenous people, I think the abusive circumstances in which many women found (and find) themselves was not sufficiently grasped and could not then be embodied in a document of this sort. Fortunately, we have moved a long way since 1948 toward understanding that the issues of gender and sexual identity involve much more than equal participation.

Professor Henkin also briefly raised the question of what to do about the oppressive side of religion itself as a human rights problem. Salman Rushdie is a casualty of religious belief and interpretation, and it is obvious that this sort of oppression cannot be isolated by blaming just one individual—the Ayatollah Khomeini. It is a broader problem. Perhaps Rushdie embodies a limit case because of the drastic response to what we in the West accept as freedom of expression. What he wrote is regarded not only as blasphemy, but apostasy, a betrayal of the given religion, the privileged birthright. So it has had a particularly traumatic effect in the world of Orthodox Islam. Many who don't share Khomeini's view do, however, believe that, given Rushdie's background, his work represents a violation of trust in relation to the Islamic community.

The final incompleteness that I want to mention (and these are not mere details in my view, but essential dimensions of an adequate foundation for a global ethic) involves the absence of any direct effort to address specific vulnerabilities of distinct identities, for instance those of gays and lesbians and others who are for some reason the targets of societal oppression. To a certain degree some of these issues have been handled subsequently in more fully elaborated human rights conventions. The Convention on the Rights of the Child, for example, was very important, because there is not enough substance in the Universal Declaration—even if conceived of as a minimal ethic—to contribute anything meaningful about the circumstances and problems of the child.

There is a second set of difficulties that I see in regard to the Universal Declaration. These are related to selectivity in its application and implementation. Operative in our general awareness of what "human rights" are about, and even in most of the academic literature on human rights, is the rather reductive assumption that human rights are really about civil and political issues only. You find scant treatment, if any, of the economic and social portions of the Universal Declaration. Yet from a textual point of view they are equally part of an organic whole. Nonetheless, governments (and the United States government especially) have not wanted to define human rights as encompassing economic and social concerns, this despite the fact that for many people in the world such concerns are a priority. As you know, there are a billion people who do not have the basic needs of life satisfied, even unto food. One of the visionary elements of the global ethic embodied in the Universal Declaration as a text is the postulate of the human right of every person on the planet to have those basic needs satisfied. But this issue has been avoided even by human rights groups. In other words, even in the nongovernmental sector, especially in the West, the main meaning of human rights, perhaps for reasons that need to be discussed, has been understood to be the struggle against torture, the struggle against genocide—the political and civil side of human rights. What we need at this stage if we are to create a universally viable global ethic is to focus on economic and social rights as deserving priority and serious attention. Unless this happens, it will always seem to most of the peoples of the world that human rights are little more than a luxury of the affluent. We can't afford to let human rights be deteriorated in this way.

Another area of selectivity in the application of the Declaration has been the degree to which governments in particular have subordinated the promotion of human rights to their strategic interests or to geopolitics. They often overlook what is done by their friends, and of course by themselves. The United States is a very interesting country in this respect because it is both very attentive to the human rights of others and also very sensitive about any criticism of itself. It has also been reluctant to commit itself to some of the central human rights instruments. It's always easy to say that human rights are for others; can we also learn to acknowledge that human rights have a relevance to ourselves? That, too, must be an aspect of an adequate universality.

Finally, I want to mention here two provisions in the Declaration that are very radical but are avoided in the literature, in statecraft, and even in the behavior of the human rights community. Article 25 says "everyone has the right to a standard of living adequate for the health and well being of himself and of his family, including food, clothing, housing, medical care, and necessary social services." Everyone has the right to an adequate standard of living. That's an extraordinary mandate, but I think it's a necessary mandate. I don't think it's something that can just be dismissed; we can't pretend it's not there. It is there, and it has to be read as part of this declaration.

In like manner, Article 28 raises what I would call the issue of world order. It says that "everyone is entitled to a social and international order in which the rights and freedoms set forth in this Declaration can be fully realized." It's questionable whether the current world order, organized as it is in terms of states and increasingly dominated by global market forces, is an international order that can actualize the economic and social rights of the peoples of the world. Is the market ethos really capable of being reconciled with a commitment to provide all people with an adequate standard of living? I have yet to see an economic assessment that convincingly reconciles an unconditional commitment to the market with this kind of ethical imperative. Until this issue is faced, there will continue to be a kind of denial on the part of human rights activists—the pretense that we can have both human rights and a market-driven world. I'm not sure that we can. At the very least we must face this issue as explicitly and honestly as possible. This need has become even more pressing with the collapse of socialism, because socialism, for all its defects, kept capitalism honest. It challenged capitalism normatively and in part triggered the impulse toward a compassionate capitalism. Without that socialist challenge, one is left with a cruel capitalism since there is no alternative, no reason to pay attention to anything but efficiency—market efficiency as revealed by aggregate measures of economic growth. That in turn marginalizes the weak and those that contribute less fully.

The only other thing I want to mention is that the 1994 Cairo conference on population and development revealed a dimension of the struggle for a global ethic based on human rights that is quite intriguing and that relates directly to the theme of this conference. One was treated to the spectacle of strange bedfellows, the Vatican and Orthodox Islam, working together in opposition to transnational, democratic grassroots groups spearheaded by the women's movement. The government representatives who were present mostly looked on, almost like confused spectators at a conference of states. The final document that emerged from the conference was a triumph for the women's movement because for the first time the issue of population balance was tied to the condition of women in society and not to some demographic quick fix. That was an enormous breakthrough on the one hand in the face of the kind of technocratic thinking that suggests that the right birth control mechanism will solve the problem, and on the other against those established religions that were trying to pretend the world isn't in a crisis and the planet isn't overcrowded. This is empowerment from below. It exists and, in my view, it is in the process of establishing a global civil society—the indispensable vehicle for the promotion of a global ethic.

It is not enough to have a text, because governments often agree to things they don't really believe in and will not implement. How do you give a text vitality in the lives of people? This has always depended on initiatives in civil society. Without Amnesty International, for example, ideas of political and civil rights would not have amounted to much, except as propaganda tools in the Cold War. They became instruments of struggle because people who saw oppression evoked these norms as the foundation for their acts. That's the kind of grassroots empowerment required for a global ethic to become real. It's a matter of transnational democracy, not just of formulating the right set of norms. Norms must become a reality in people's lives.

The great potential in world religions is that they can reach peoples around the globe more directly and more fully than any other societal institution. If the religions of the world, despite their diversity, could begin to educate people based on their diverse interpretations of the Universal Declaration, it would eventually have an enormous impact on daily life, on people's sense of what their own entitlements are, *and* on the meaning of citizenship, and state/society relations generally. I don't think we should discount the potential for this progressive role of religion, though we need to remain sensitive to its regressive sides as well.

Panel #2

• • •

PERSPECTIVES ON A GLOBAL ETHIC AND COMMON VALUES

• • •

Sissela Bok
Harvard Center for Population and Development Studies

Robert A.F. Thurman
Department of Religion, Columbia University

Mark Juergensmeyer (Panelist and Moderator)
Department of Sociology, University of California, Santa Barbara

Panel #2 Presentation by

SISSELA BOK

• • •

Sissela Bok, a writer and philosopher, was born in Sweden and educated in Switzerland and France before coming to the United States. She received her PhD in philosophy at Harvard in 1970. Formerly a professor of philosophy at Brandeis University, she is currently a Distinguished Fellow at the Harvard Center for Population and Development Studies. Her books include Lying: Moral Choice in Private and Public Life, Secrets: On the Ethics of Concealment and Revelation, A Strategy for Peace: Human Values and the Threat of War *and* Alva Myrdal: A Daughter's Memoir.

I am delighted to be here today. I think it's especially important that we try to bring together both the secular and the religious perspectives. Too often efforts to consider global values, universal values, are pursued exclusively in a religious context or in a secular context. Here we're going to try to do it together.

I actually had a worm's eye perspective on the creation of the Universal Declaration. In 1947, when I was a young girl, I moved to Geneva with my parents who worked for the United Nations. I went to the International School there, and I was what you might call a "UN brat." The parents of many of the children in the school were in the UN, and since those were the days when the Declaration was being formulated, Mrs. Eleanor Roosevelt

> "It's extremely important that all over the world groups are meeting to see what can be done, what one can formulate, to try to put forth a minimalist set of values, and also to debate the various forms that maximalist values take."

---

* © Sissela Bok, 1995.

and many other people came to speak about it. We had a real sense of the tremendous excitement of the time—of the potential, the great opportunities that were present after the war.

I strongly agree with Professor Henkin in one particular regard. I, too, think that the 1948 Declaration on Human Rights is a key text. It's one of those foundational documents that we need to know about and study when we think about a vast topic such as global ethics. However, I don't exactly agree with him that it is a minimal document. I think we need to move further towards a minimum in order to be able to cross all the religious and cultural boundaries that we must cross if we are going to arrive at a document that everyone can actually agree on. As we all know, in 1947 and 1948 the Cold War began, then the nuclear balance of terror came about, but the work on human rights through international law continued because of organizations like Amnesty International and the growing human rights movement. Nonetheless, there was a sense that things were not moving at all as fast as they could, in part because there were so many oppressive governments doing all they could to deny human rights.

Then, in 1989, there was again a mood similar to the one in '48, a sense of the potential the human rights movement and declarations related to human rights might have. At the time, however, there were already twice as many human beings on earth as there had been in 1948; five billion instead of two and a half billion. That meant that the number of human beings whose rights were to be respected according to such a document had doubled, and, as we know, many of them lived and continue to live in abject poverty. But now, in 1994, only five years later, I think there is much greater anguish and bewilderment in the human rights community. I know that all of you feel it too. For instance, if we think of the letters that members of Amnesty International have written so magnificently for decades to oppressive governments, we might ponder exactly to whom one could write in Rwanda where more than a million people have had their human rights desperately injured and between 500,000 and a million have actually been killed. What we see in Rwanda and other places are so-called complex humanitarian emergencies. They're complex because they're not the kind of emergencies that might arise after an earthquake or a flood. They're complex because they have been made worse by human beings who have deliberately inflicted suffering on others and interfered with the humanitarian aid that could otherwise have come from abroad.

We now have staggering numbers of people the world over who are killed or wounded and homeless. Four decades ago 50 percent of war-related casualties were civilian. Now it's 90 percent, and a great many of them are children. Because of the discouragement, and because human rights are very much on the defensive, there are books coming out such as the one by the German theorist Hans Magnus Enzensberger, called *Civil Wars*. The book aroused a great deal of debate in Europe. Enzensberger argues that there's more talk than ever about human rights, and yet there are more people than ever suffering the most abject deprivation of their human rights. And so, he says, it's all rhetoric. He would also probably say that what we are doing here is useless. According to Enzensberger, there is an epidemic spreading around the world, not only in societies such as those in the ex-Yugoslavia and Rwanda, but also in our own inner cities. He compares serial killers, graffiti vandals, and mass murderers, abroad and at home, and says they represent a kind of virus of civil war that is spreading the world over. He believes there is nothing the international community can do. All that we can hope for is to work at some very local level and try to do our best to repair some of the damage done by these civil wars.

There are also a great many people—there have been for some decades—who in the name of relativism say that it's useless to come together in a meeting like this. There are so many different cultures, with such different values, that it is, unfortunately, impossible to have anything in common and so, also very unfortunately, it is impossible to do very much for the people one sees suffering in other nations. There is also a great deal of blaming going on; by secular people, for instance, who reproach members of religious traditions, especially because of the so-called holy wars and all the killing that goes on in their name, but also by many religious people who believe that it's those godless, secular ones who are bringing about much of the destruction in the world.

There are many forces converging today that could wipe out the kind of concern with human rights that we have here and that has existed during much of this century. And yet it's so very clear that the problems in the world are collective, that the responses have to be collective, and on a global basis. It's also clear that the problems that exist the world over have not been carefully separated and dealt with as either religious or secular. They are all intermingled—as we can see for instance right now in Bosnia. So the responses also need to combine the secular and the religious.

I have been writing for some years about the search for shared values, values that can be shared across all boundaries, cultural, religious and all others.* I arrived at the conclusion that what we would need as a starting point are what I call minimalist values: values that are already known everywhere, whether or not people abide by them. There are certain values that are already recognized everywhere, and that have always been, because even the tiniest village or society could not survive if there were no constraints at all on, for example, killing, breaking promises, or lying. These have had to arise for the purposes of survival—of families, of communities—long before there were established religions and long before there were political systems like democracy, much less a United Nations. And I suggest that all societies have had to find a way to formulate these very minimal values, for instance, that of mutual care and reciprocity which all societies understand with regard to bringing up children, or in honoring fathers and mothers. At the same time certain moral constraints such as those on killing, on lying, on breaking promises had to be formulated, as well as what Stuart Hampshire, in his book, *Innocence and Experience*, calls a kind of rudimentary justice, a sense of justice that existed long before we had courts, long before we had institutions to work on justice. People have pointed out that in every society there is a sense of injustice among children if one child is punished for what another has done. The child who's punished knows that it's unfair; you don't need to have gone to law school for that. All of these minimal values are ones that are broadly recognized. You not only know about them in your own community, you know when they are violated in another community.

At the same time, of course, that's not all that we need. In every community and in every family, as well as in most religions, maximalist values are worked out that are also very important. We couldn't live with just the minimalist position; we need to work out our own set of values. We may draw on some religion, some political system, or some philosopher, or we may work them out on our own, but we need those

---

*See Sissela Bok, *Common Values*, forthcoming from University of Missouri Press, Winter 1995.

maximalist values. They may not be readily shared, but in advocating them, one can compare and debate them. For instance, we can debate everything that is proposed as a part of a Declaration of Human Rights. But then other people might say, why are you just talking about human rights here? Why not animals, too? That is a question that is important to some people but not others. It may not be part of most discussions about minimalist values, but it's very important to a great many people.

While writing about all this last year, I was especially interested in the many efforts made on an international level to arrive at common statements of values. For instance, the United Nations meeting on human rights in Vienna last year. Also, the Parliament of the World's Religions. Here today, we're studying their declaration, *Towards a Global Ethic.* There was also the encyclical by Pope John-Paul II, *Veritatus Splendor,* the splendor of truth. The Pope begins with a quite minimalist restatement of five of the Ten Commandments, adds "love thy neighbor as thyself," and then moves on in a direction I find quite maximalist. This is his own maximalist position, but he puts it before us for debate. There is also an ongoing project by the United Nations Commission on Global Governance. It aims to develop a statement on values that would cross all boundaries. And, as I have found out here today, there is a project that has been going on in my hometown, Cambridge, as well as in New York: the *Project on Religion and Human Rights.*

There have been many efforts, then. They offer a tremendous counterweight to people like Hans Magnus Enzensberger, who says it's all worthless, that it can't be done, that we mustn't even try it. It's extremely important that all over the world groups are meeting to see what can be done, what one can formulate, to try to put forth a minimalist set of values, and also to debate the various forms that maximalist values take.

I think we need to study the document produced by the June 1993 United Nations World Conference on Human Rights, too. It's very important to look at the 1948 Declaration, but we need to look at the 1993 document because more than any other, perhaps, it reveals the extraordinary range and depth of disagreement about human rights on the part of various governments. Here it's important to distinguish between the governments that participated and the representatives of grassroots organizations who were there as well. One of the important questions that was asked was what exactly we mean by group rights. Another was if, and when, group rights can override individual rights. What about rights that are violated by governments in another country? Do we have the right, or perhaps the duty, to cross borders and try to rectify the situation? And what about rights violated in the home, the rights of women, for instance, or of children, whether in our own countries or abroad? What obligations do we have there?

In the 1993 document, for the first time, there was genuine emphasis on the denial of rights to women, even in their own homes. Some people said that this was just an effort to be politically correct, that you had to somehow say more about women than you did in the past. But I think that assumption is quite wrong. What was demonstrated in Vienna is that when promulgating rather vague declarations on human rights in the past, it had been taken for granted that women might be counted, but that one didn't need to look at what was actually happening to women around the world. It became clear that these rights would have to be stated much more carefully. And it was understood that, when we talk about the right not to be tortured, we also have in mind the right not to have an abortion performed on us against our will. When we talk about the right not to be imprisoned, that also means not being imprisoned in one's own home.

A number of governments, led by those of China, Indonesia, and Malaysia, argued that there should be a tradeoff between economic well-being and the full-scale political rights that they called "Western" ideas. They claimed that poor people, if they're sufficiently poor, really don't care much about voting. They care simply about having food. But I think the philosopher and economist, Amartya Sen, has made it clear that those political rights which may not seem so important are in fact fundamentally important in order to avoid famine and starvation. He has pointed out that the great famine in China that caused between forty and fifty million deaths could take place only because there was no free press, no right to vote, to express your view, and no right even to learn from other villages whether people elsewhere were starving as much. So, every village in China could imagine that its inhabitants were the only ones in this dire, dire state.

I think the argument that political rights don't count as much as economic rights is wrongly formulated. The Vienna declaration did indeed affirm the right to development, but it also pointed out that this right could never be invoked to justify abridging internationally recognized human rights. That's important; it's crucial to argue this point. Otherwise, oppressive governments would say, "we are doing all these things—torturing people, putting them in prison, etc.—for the sake of the overriding right to development."

At least this declaration says you can't do that. At the same time, it is really rather peculiar to say that you can never abridge any right at all for the sake of a desperate need for development of your own nation. Countries do that all the time, in fact. So perhaps the most problematic aspect of this 1993 document was clause five, which stated that all human rights are universal, indivisible, interdependent, and interrelated. Yes, they're universal, yes, they are interrelated, but indivisible? Are we really prepared to say that? Are we really willing to say, for instance, that the right to free holidays with pay or to a certain standard of living for an extraordinarily rapidly mounting world population is completely indivisible from the right not to be tortured? If so, not even the richest country in the world could totally satisfy the expectation.

Now, the Parliament of the World's Religions, which formulated the document entitled *Towards a Global Ethic*, invites us readers to take part in the debate at meetings like this. It specifically says that it is not a final document. That declaration, however, much like the 1993 Vienna declaration, confusingly blends together the absolute minimum expected for any human being and all kinds of maximalist ideas, some of which are very noble, but definitely not shared. For instance, the declaration sets forth the Golden Rule which has cropped up in every society in some form, but then it says that this is an irrevocable, unconditional norm for all areas of life—for families, communities, races, nations, and religions. This is not the way that rule was framed by Hillel or by Confucius, two of its earliest formulators. The document then goes on to interpret this rule in a very idiosyncratic way, to say that the Golden Rule rejects every form of egoism, all forms of selfishness whether individual or collective—there goes the right to development—whether in the form of class thinking, race thinking, nationalism, or sexism. Now that would mean that any human being who ever had a selfish thought would be in great trouble.

The Declaration goes on to enumerate four broad and ancient guidelines for human behavior thought to come from the Golden Rule, in ways that are not specified: commitment to a culture of nonviolence and respect for life, commitment to a culture of solidarity and a just economic order, commitment to a culture of tolerance and a life of truthfulness, commitment to a culture of equal rights and partnership between men and women. There are also many admirable principles in what comes under each of these four guidelines. But you'll notice that some of these principles are minimalist ones that people in every society would have heard about, while others many wouldn't have heard about at all—for instance, the "just economic order" the document proposes, or the culture of equal rights and partnership between men and women. These are maximalist ideals. I would agree with them, but you cannot simply say they exist everywhere and can be understood by everyone.

In any case, it's very good that we're going to be discussing this document here, because we need to see the different levels on which it operates—see what might be agreed to everywhere and what might not be but really should be, and remember that those two possibilities are very, very different.

Finally, the declaration is festooned with needless rhetoric. For instance, it holds that there should be no new global order without a new global ethic. Elsewhere it says there will be no new ethic; rather, there will be an ethic that's recognized everywhere, that can be found in the Ten Commandments, in Buddhist literature, and elsewhere. I think one has to make a choice, and I would argue that it's too late for a new ethic. We'd better move along with the ethic that we have had in the past and try to improve on it. Of course, there will have to be extensions, and new formulations of whatever it is we begin with as our minimalist ethic.

The document also ends with a call for a global transformation of consciousness. As a secular person, this worries me. It is not at all a call designed to enlist agreement among the more than 20 percent of humanity that claims to have no religious allegiance, or among the many religious persons who are wary of that kind of transformation. There will also be difficulty with the claim that the set of core values is to be found only in the world's religions. It must be made clear that the core values are also found in secular texts and indeed were in existence long before there were any texts at all. In the age-old debate about whether something is right because God declared it to be right or whether God declared it to be right because it was right, it's very important not to come down squarely on one side without at least acknowledging that the other exists. That again is part of the debate that should be taking place.

Well, the aim of the two documents I've been discussing—to seek broad-based agreement on basic values—is praiseworthy, and it's very important that this debate should go on. But if we're going to avoid the kind of skepticism that comes from people like Hans Magnus Enzensberger (whose book, by the way, I do recommend as a real challenge to a meeting such as ours), if we're going to overcome the critique by people convinced of cultural relativism, and if we're going to overcome the barrier between secular and religious efforts, then we will have to carry the debate further and separate carefully what is minimalist from what is maximalist. We must work from both directions and see where we can agree, how much farther we might actually be able to go than we might otherwise have gone. And it is more urgent than ever to do so given the way crises such as that in Rwanda are reaching into other nations as well.

I want to end with the word chosen by Dr. Samuel Johnson when he talked about values needing to be applied. By "applied," he meant "put to the use of life." If we're really going to put these global values to the use of life, if they're not just going to be words, then we will need an approach that is more discriminating about the minimalist and the maximalist perspectives, more understanding of where in religion and in secular traditions these values arise. That is to say, an approach more aimed at bringing theory and practice together as a means of putting values to the use of life.

Panel #2 Presentation by

ROBERT A.F. THURMAN

• • •

Robert A.F. Thurman is Jey Tsong Khapa Professor on Indo-Tibetan Buddhism at Columbia University and Chairperson of the Department of Religion. After receiving his PhD in Sanskrit and Indian Studies from Harvard University in 1972, he taught at Amherst College and Boston University. Professor Thurman is a founding trustee of the American Institute of Buddhist Studies.

Again, let me welcome everyone here on behalf of the Department of Religion. A department of religion in a liberal arts and sciences research university is automatically in the "world religion business." Most of us are philosophers of some sort or another who wandered beyond the confines of modern Western thought and became fascinated by one or the other philosophy of a different civilization. In making a teaching career in that area, we function in a climate of constant, at least two-pronged dialogue. On the one hand with modernity and various sciences, and on the other hand with the other world traditions and their home civilizations. Some of us are also always concerned with a third area: the application of all of these ideas and phenomena to life, as Dr. Bok said, which means to ethics, not only in thought but also in practice. And that means that we worry systematically about the current world crisis, the current world confusion and the ongoing

"The world religions should work together by asking each other to live up to some of their founding impulses and to overcome some of their bureaucratic, contradictory tenets which are in many cases oppressive of their own founding impulses."

world apocalypse. I don't think it's something we're waiting for; I think it's clearly something that is happening. Rwanda, Bosnia, Sarajevo, Tibet, it's all going on as we speak.

So we are delighted that the Boston Research Center for the 21st Century has made this conference possible in benighted New York, bringing colleagues from various disciplines together with professionals who work on the front lines of this area. If the tiniest little fragment of what we consider here today has any relevance, if it ameliorates any activity bearing on the well-being of even a single human, it will have been well worth the effort.

The questions I will work on today, as an American Buddhist philosopher worried about the world, are the following:

• What is the UN's primary function? Is it the protection of people and their environment where national governments do not hold sway or may even pose the threat?

• Will the UN be able to perform its function effectively in the longer run without being empowered in at least some areas as an effective world government? Could the UN become such a world government without gaining the full blessing and cooperation of the world religions?

• Could the world religions confer full legitimacy on such an organization in concert with all the other religions and with the various forms of secularism? That would mean, of course, each religion's de facto acceptance of the coequal status of other religions and even secular humanism itself approached as a major world religion.

As an amateur, let me rehearse my thinking on these questions. The UN was formed by the victorious allied powers at the end of the last all-out world war while they were fresh in their acknowledgment that they had catastrophically failed on their own to keep the peace. As soon as it was founded, the more powerful nations took steps to retain control of its agenda and not to accord it the legitimacy of a body that directly represents the people of the entire globe. In its half century of operation, it has done much good in many areas, although politically it served as a forum of verbal combat between the great powers during the Cold War. It has not realized, therefore, the dream underlying its founding, not because most nations are so attached to their sovereignty in all areas, but because the imperial, and what I call post-imperial, big powers will not submit any aspects of their operations to its control.

I am hopeful that this will soon change, since all but one—and the one I refer to is China—of these big powers have by now given up their imperial pretensions.

There is some hope that, after renunciation of military territorial imperialism has become universal, the big powers and all nations will decide to hire the UN to keep the peace between them, in the way in which the first king was hired in ancient mythology as the one who could protect his people from each other. In the language of the Buddhist sutras, the UN would become *mahasammata*, the "elected one," the first king. But then a new problem would surely ensue. Once the UN had real power even to a limited degree, particular national governments would resist intensely were it to act against their individual interests. They would always suspect that the politics internal to the newly empowered UN were being manipulated by their enemies, and so they would quickly look for ways to take back whatever measure of sovereignty they had ceded to it in a moment of heady idealism, perhaps coming from a conference such as this.

Obviously, such nations will never continue to empower the UN until the people of those nations insist that the UN has more legitimacy concerning their rights and their lives, in some areas at least, than their own national government does. To do this, the people of the world will have to come to a new understanding of sovereignty, what we might call an internationally democratic notion of the sovereignty of the people over certain fundamental things. They must come to feel that the nations have lost the right to represent them in those areas where they feel the United Nations can do a better job. These areas will surely include: 1) the preservation of the environment, land, forests, oceans, fresh water bodies, atmosphere, and food and energy resources; 2) preservation of their individual human rights against the coercive activities of their local elites and governments; 3) protection against the depredations of multinational corporations, particularly arms merchants as well as resource and product monopolists with international scale and supranational economic power; and 4) assurance of their access to uncensored global information networks. There are these four at least, but I'm sure that others who have thought more carefully about it will give us a longer list.

When we look for a viable world in the twenty-first century, we must look to a UN with at least these capabilities. But then the question arises: What idea, event, entity or institution could possibly push the world's people towards acceptance of the UN's global sovereignty in at least these four crucial areas? And here's where the modernists and the secularists on their own will get stuck. They might point to the Internet, to satellite TV, to telephone, to travel, and so on, but it is still a fact that the local governments can limit access to these whenever they deem it necessary to maintain their power and to hide their oppressive activities. We saw them pull the plug at Tiananmen Square, and we saw the media grovel to get the plug reattached subsequently. We've been seeing it since then. These technological connecting strands are immensely useful and potentially liberative, but by themselves they cannot create the popular planetary shift we need.

I think it is clear that only the collective institutions of the world religions can accomplish this task, should they decide they wish to do so. They have actually never felt the urge for the most part, preferring rather to maintain their local alliances with national governments and to persist in all-out competition with one another whenever feasible. There are still strong elements of global triumphalism in the world religions' institutions. We must face this unpleasant fact if we are going to come up with any workable prospect of getting them to cooperate in this hour of dire necessity. This is where the concept of a viable global ethic comes in. I think Professor Bok's minimalist suggestions are most appropriate in this context. The task becomes at the start one of drawing the leaders of the world religions' central institutions into a sustained dialogue over the question of what minimal ethical principles all of them could accept, disregarding their intractable variety of religious and ideological foundations of these principles. And here I would add that secular humanism should be included as one of the world religions.

I believe that the minimal ethical principles we seek may be reflected in certain rights and responsibilities of individuals and institutions:

• The right to human consideration and the responsibility of kindness. No one can reject this in most cases.

• The right to gentle and realistic treatment and the responsibility to restrain violence and manifest truthfulness.

• The right to just treatment and the responsibility to restrain power for the sake of long-term fairness and legitimacy. Professor Bok has thought this through well, it seems to me, and I look forward to her book.

His Holiness the Dalai Lama always speaks so movingly, as many of you I'm sure have heard, when he is asked about his religion. He always talks about how it isn't really Buddhism; his primary religion is what he calls the common human religion, which is kindness. And whenever he does that, of course, it always gets to people. Unfortunately, he's never been able to present that message to the UN because of the fact that the big powers dominate the agenda of the UN in an improper manner, and won't invite him.

In this light I wanted to say one thing as a footnote in relation to what Professor Henkin said. As he described quite accurately, members of the liberal, secular, capitalist, democratic, scientific human rights community have an image of themselves creating the Universal Declaration of Human Rights by breaking away from the world religions and almost in opposition to the world religions. They chose to talk about belief and muted the mention of religion, knowing of the contentiousness of the world religions. On the other hand, if we're not to despair of enlisting in this kind of effort the world religions, whether it be Islamic, Jain, Buddhist, Confucian, Christian, or Jewish members of the world populations, we have to distinguish between that common religiosity and that dogmatic and politically oriented set of tenets and doctrines of the governing bodies of these religions. I feel somehow we have to take back the definitions and the analysis of these religions from the dominant elites of those religions.

We have to remember that all the founders of the great world religions, usually at the outset, were strung up on some unpleasant place or persecuted by the existing bosses of the dominant religions. Therefore, the liberal idea of world religions as enjoining duties on people only and not giving them rights is a little distorted in the sense that it accepts the definitions of religions as dictated by the governing institutions. Christianity, once it became the church of Rome and hence part of the establishment, changed a lot of its doctrines from the time when it had been a revolutionary and an individually based spiritual movement. Buddha was an arch rebel against the Vedas and was in peril of his life at many times when he said, "That business of offering those animals into the fire in sacrifice is really an error—the animals don't like it, and it's not actually helping you much. Instead, you should do something about kindness to the animals and to the living beings around you." He was, in fact, a rebel and perceived as anti-religious by the established religions in his day. Mahavira, founder of Jainism, was not at the time of the founding talking about duties. He was talking about rights of the individual to liberation, to freedom from suffering and coercion and oppression by governments, as well as coercion and oppression by idiotic ideas in general.

We should not concede the definition of religions to be determined by those who presently are in power in religious institutions. The world religions should work together by asking each other to live up to some of their founding impulses and to overcome some of their bureaucratic, contradictory tenets which are, in many cases, oppressive of their own founding impulses. Therefore, liberal secular human rights people need the help of world religion scholars to analyze the strands within different religions and thereby be able to separate out from the dogmas of a reigning religious ruler the original teachings of the religious founders. This would be a challenge to the religions to live up to their higher ideals in our apocalyptic situation.

If the world religions, after such systematic dialogue, were to decide that they need the protection of something like the UN against the abuses of power of national governments, just think of the power of their influence over the people of this planet! Internet and the information superhighway may be great, but there already exists a huge internet consisting of the temple, the monastery, the church, the mosque, the synagogue, and the university (in fact, the church of the liberal-secular-scientific-democratic humanist.) There are sacred spots in or near every village, town, and city in this world. Indigenous peoples have their sacred spots where their shamans and their leaders stay. Larger communities have a plurality of these religious institutions. Here in New York we have a festival of all the world religions on every level of practice, and a bunch of new ones in between, manifesting themselves spontaneously in Times Square. And the great Communist countries have been unable to restrain the resurgence of the powerful human demand for some spiritual satisfaction, or at least solace.

If the highest governing bodies of all these religious organizations felt pressure from the world community and their own followers and from a more critical understanding of the nature of religion, they might be constrained to issue new interpretations, new edicts, and new counsels to their clergy. The message that would thus go from town to town would be one of a sensible and practical cooperation among the religions. It would be a message of a unified determination by all of them that the atrocious behavior of tyrants, despots, bullies, and bandits, no matter what sort of legitimacy they're wrapping themselves in, will no longer be tolerated. And that the people of the world will act through their global representatives at the UN to guarantee a minimum security and opportunity to all individuals.

I am aware that this vision is utopian at the moment, but then again the moment is apocalyptic in all of its various senses. I am also aware that what is called the fundamentalist tendency in all the religions is working in just the opposite direction to this vision, and is perhaps more powerful at the moment. I have specific ideas about how we have let this atavistic tendency grow by our own neglect and complacency. And there is a very direct way to ameliorate it, which is to demand that people live up to the founding impulses of their various religions, which we have every right to do. Suppose some mad cult leader who has a certain interpretation of some religion says that, because his followers say they're a religion, out of religious tolerance we have to let them do whatever they want. I think this is a kind of excessive impracticality on the part of liberalism, and is really unnecessary. Once they're violating the basic human religion of kindness, then I think we have a right to remind them of the precepts of kindness inevitably found in the sayings of the founders of all the great world religions.

I have thrown out this ball of ideas, this positive vision, however utopian, just to put it in play, so to speak. I look forward to the day's discussion. Thank you very much.

Panel #2 Presentation by

MARK JUERGENSMEYER

• • •

Mark Juergensmeyer is Professor of Sociology and Chair of the Global Peace and Security Program at the University of California, Santa Barbara. He holds a PhD in political science from the University of California, Berkeley, a Master's of Divinity from Union Theological Seminary and a Master's from Columbia University's School of International Affairs. His honors include fellowships at the Woodrow Wilson International Center for Scholars and the United States Institute of Peace.

L et me begin by telling you about some projects that I've been involved in that are somewhat similar to the project that you're engaged in now—looking at the possibility of a global ethic as a basis for undergirding a broad gamut of human values, especially those enshrined in the United Nations' Universal Declaration of Human Rights. Some fifteen years ago, Bob Thurman and I were both involved in a project that I had the privilege of codirecting, the Berkeley-Harvard Program for the Comparative Study of Values. We deliberately called it *values* rather than *ethics* because even then we were somewhat queasy about terms, and especially about what the term *ethics* might signify. In fact, there was a great deal of discussion among those of us who were organizing the project as to whether ethics was really the right term, or whether it was so laden with Western values and assumptions that it really couldn't apply comparatively, especially to the

"We must work toward a convocation of human virtues, human values, and human dignity that encompasses all of the traditions, including our own, which is seen by many people in other traditions as culturally narrow as is theirs."

great Asian traditions. So our first conference was really a pair of conferences, the first at Berkeley when we asked the question, are there ethics in the Asian traditions? And at the second conference at Harvard when the question was, is there dharma in the West? We tried to take an analogous term, the dharmic tradition, and ask whether there was a common sense of dharmic values, responsibility, and collective virtues in the Western tradition.

From the very beginning the group was badly split between what came to be known as the universalist and the comparativist positions. The universalists were those scholars among us, led by Sumner Twiss, Ronald Green, and David Little, who were trying to argue that you could conceive of a universalist ethics based upon categories of analysis developed under the Western philosophic tradition, especially Kant. And then there were those of us, the comparativists, including Don Swearer at Swarthmore, Jack Hawley now at Columbia, Bob Thurman, and Mark Juergensmeyer, who argued just as vigorously that you had to start at the other extreme, that you had to start where people are in their living traditions and try to build up some sense of a collectivity of shared values. The universalists regarded us as hopeless relativists, and we, of course, regarded them as simple universalists.

But there were some significant moments in this discussion where the two camps were forced to face the conclusion that maybe we shared more than we initially thought. I remember one poignant moment when we were discussing suttee, the tradition within Hinduism where the widow throws herself on the funeral pyre of her dead husband. This is a rare event and yet it's a dramatic one, and it's often regarded as the litmus test of the universalization of values. At one of our conferences we were discussing that act in its social context and the British response to it when Peter Berger, a sociologist from Boston University, leapt up and said, "Look! Is there a single one of you—if there were a suttee being committed in this room, if there were a funeral pyre and the tragic woman was being placed upon the coals—is there a single one of you who would not leap up and drag her from the fire?" And, of course, he was right. There wasn't a single one of us, with whatever universalist, relativist, comparatist values, who didn't have a sense of the dignity of life and humanity and who, despite whatever explanations were given for her acts, would not drag that poor woman from the fire.

Thus, our project concluded that there was a core of shared values throughout the world, and we produced a number of books that tried to explore this core. We attempted to look not only at codes of ethics and the codification of virtues, but also at eminent figures, since the ethics and virtues of traditions are transmitted as much by great heroes and saints as they are by any practical rule of living or by laws of behavior enshrined by any collectivity. One of the books, *Saints and Virtues*, edited by Jack Hawley and published by the University of California Press, explored the phenomenon—nearly universal—of sainthood. *Cosmogony and Ethics*, edited by Frank Reynolds and Robin Lovin for the University of Chicago Press, looked at the myths of creation as a model for various kinds of shared assumptions, especially about our relationship to the environment. A volume on economic ethics in Theravada Buddhism was co-edited by Don Swearer and Russell Sizemore. *Speaking of Truth*, a volume edited by Diana Eck, emerged from the first convocation of women from various religious traditions that dealt with the rights of women from the point of view of those traditions. And then there was a large project, a volume that John Carman and I edited—*A Bibliographical Guide to the Comparative Study of Ethics*, published by Cambridge University Press. Although prohibitively expensive, it is meant to be a basic guide to understanding the ethical traditions—and the themes that cut across them—that would help one envision the possibility of a shared global ethic.

The second project I want to tell you about aimed at bringing together the strands of consensus that had begun to emerge from the first. This was a conference on religion and human rights, sponsored by Columbia University, in which I was asked to participate several years after the Berkeley-Harvard project. The conference was interested as much in the problem that religion creates for human rights as it was in the way in which human rights is undergirded by religious traditions. I was struck by the fact that at this conference David Little talked about Islam and the human rights tradition within the Islamic value system. Sumner B. Twiss took up sociobiology and the attempt to look within the biological character of humanity for the basis for a cooperative ethics, a basis for a minimalist set of values based simply on shared species concerns. They had moved away from an exclusive concern with the Western philosophical tradition, just as those of us who were comparativists were determined not to be stuck within the relativist

camp, not to be put in the position of saying, well, Hindus value suttee, therefore we wouldn't reach up and grab that poor woman on the
burning pyre.

After all, every single religious tradition affirms not only its peculiar version of truth but the universality of truth itself. There is not a
single religious tradition that doesn't to some extent claim to have a
window on a larger and global sense of virtue and well-being. If that's
the case, they all must affirm that in some way, somehow, other traditions also provide glimpses towards that same vision.

The most recent project I want to tell you about is a personal one,
the one that I've been engaged in for the last ten years or so that led to
the book *The New Cold War? Religious Nationalism Confronts the Secular
State*. This has been a troubling book for me to write because, as some-
body who has always been interested in religion and politics and has
always seen religion as a resource for what is virtuous and good within
public morality, it has been disturbing in the last ten years or so to see
the vicious spiral of violence that has emerged between religious communities and secular political orders. There should, after all, be some
basic and deeply shared convictions about the morality of public institutions. And yet today religion has become a problem for human rights.

There is no doubt in my mind that the reason the Parliament of the
World's Religions produced its statement, *Towards a Global Ethic*, was
in large part to counteract the public sentiment that religion is a problem for human rights and for social order. Things like this don't come
in a vacuum, they come because people are concerned in this case about
the way in which religion is presented. When I look down the list of
the signators of that statement, I see religious persons united across
faiths. But they are a certain kind of liberal religious person, and their
inclusion in this list indicates the fact that, within every religious tradition, there is increasingly a polarization between liberals and fundamentalists. As much as anything else, this was a parliament of liberal
spokespersons for religious traditions. Sadly, they have more in common with liberals in other religions than most of them have with their
compatriots at the fundamentalist extreme of their own religious traditions. So for us the questions are: What do the liberal wings of religions have in common in supporting human rights, and what do the
fundamentalist wings have in common in opposing human rights? And
how can we discover resources within religious traditions for uniting

people who are of the same faith but at polar ends of the spectrum on issues that are so important for so many of us?

The last chapter of my book, *The New Cold War?*, is on religion and human rights. I try to see some way out of the problem that any traditional, communitarian vision of morality necessarily has with modern enlightenment values that emphasize individual rights and responsibilities over the collectivity. Much of the problem that traditionalists have with human rights is *rights*—the notion that individuals can possess a greater power for moral clarity than do collectivities. Nowhere was this demonstrated more boldly than in that difficult moment early on in the hostage crisis after students had taken over the American Embassy in Teheran. Jimmy Carter, trying to appeal to the moral sentiments of the Ayatollah Khomeini said (and I paraphrase), "Dear sir, don't you realize that this action has violated international law and universal human rights?" And the response that came back was chilling. He said, "Mr. Carter, Islam is human rights. You're claiming the universality of your tradition. But Islam is human rights."

We need to accept the fact that for many people in other traditions on the fundamentalist end of the spectrum the resources within those traditions are a better basis for the universality of ethics than are the proud proclamations of our own tradition of human rights. Until we understand this, I think there will be deep difficulties in overcoming this impasse. The road out is precisely the one Sissela Bok has been discussing. We must work toward a convocation of human virtues, human values, and human dignity that encompasses all of the traditions, including our own, which is seen by many people in other traditions as culturally narrow as is theirs.

Is this ethical consensus possible? I'm struck when I read the constitution of the Islamic Republic of Iran—a document that you might not peruse as carefully as the UN Declaration of Human Rights, but you probably should. I am struck by the degree to which this document, so identified with the Ayatollah Khomeini and the revolution in Iran, is more consistent with the UN Declaration of Human Rights than is the list of human rights in our own American Constitution. It includes rights we haven't even thought of adding to the US Constitution—rights for women, for example. The American states were not able to reach a consensus on this issue, but it is in the Constitution of the Islamic Republic of Iran. The right of people to a decent job, to free education, medical care—something that the Clinton administration was not able to bring about with our own Congress—are included in the Constitution of the Islamic Republic of Iran. It is a pristine model of constitutional support for human rights, and the only thing that might give us pause is the occasional caveat that one finds within the constitution: "subject to the principles of Islam." Is this caveat the opening of Pandora's box, from which all sorts of limitations to human rights may fly? Proponents of Baha'i would certainly think so. Proponents of certain other Islamic sects might think so. But the point is that there is at least a basis for forming an accord between the most deeply held fundamentalist religious sentiments and what we proudly see within our own tradition as virtues worthy of universalist subscription. Yet this accord is possible only if we are careful to avoid the presumption that our own fairly recent historico-philosophic tradition has the sole resources for moral thinking with this kind of universal clarity and vision.

The last view I'd like to offer you today is the one out the window. If you look outside, there's a glorious urban landscape. The most dramatic views on the horizon are the Empire State Building and the Chrysler Building, symbols of secular pride. But there's also the unfinished Cathedral of Saint John the Divine and its angel with the trumpet. It's a skyline like that of virtually every city—punctuated by symbols of secular and religious affiliations. If we look carefully, we might see other churches, other spires, synagogues, Muslim minarets, Buddhist, Sikh, and Hindu temples. The landscape from this distant view is one of separateness. There is a static quality to the scene. But if we look down to the street level, we find just people. There are people of all kinds, and they go to Korean grocery stores, they get into cabs with Sikh cab drivers, they exist in constant interaction in an increasingly plural world with peoples whose views are quite different from their own. And my guess is that long before universal declarations of human rights are instituted everywhere, and long before parliaments of religions proclaim a universal global ethic for all, people in their pluralism, in their daily interaction, will find a way of getting along—not just because they want to, but because they have to in a world that's becoming less and less an aggregate of separate things and entities, and increasingly a unified flow of peoples.

OPEN DISCUSSION
Following Panel #2

Benjamin Ferencz: About fifty years ago at Nuremberg I was responsible for prosecuting twenty-two educated men, members of the Einsatzgruppe, for having murdered a million people. They murdered these people because they didn't share the religion of the group in power. All Jews were to be killed—men, women and children—without hesitation, dropped into a ditch. The same was to happen to the gypsies. These men shared a common ethic even though their religions were different. Some were Catholics, some were Protestants; there were no Jews of course. Their ethic promised a better world. There was nothing I could do to persuade them that they were wrong. Since that time I've been trying to change the nature of that kind of a world and have been much involved in the problems you're discussing here and have written many books on them.

You regard a global ethic optimistically when you say people have things which will enable them to go on and manage, but if you look at Rwanda and Yugoslavia, that seems to be a very doubtful proposition.

So let me suggest something specific, drawing on the utopian idealism described by Professor Thurman. I don't think it's utopian to plan a better world, one where we share a minimal ethic, whether it be called sharing or togetherness or human dignity. That's not unrealistic. We have set up a legal structure to do that, and it's the United Nations. We have designated the Security Council as the agency which we have empowered to maintain peace and security for all individuals. We have not given it the tools or the rules to do that job, but it can be done. May I suggest we try to make that work as best we can. It will be imperfect surely, but if we start by rejecting that or begin with new philosophical concepts in hopes of a better world, we will not see the progress that we all hope for.

[Unidentified]: There are some things that to my mind are missing from today's discussion, and I'd like to have them considered somehow. One involves the dignity of the cosmos as propounded by indigenous populations of the United States before Columbus got here. A second missing element seems to be the psychodynamics, the origins of hate and love as defined and analyzed by Melanie Klein and illustrated by C. Fred Alford. There are also two volumes entitled the *Psychodynamics of International Relations*, which offer an absolutely fundamental theory on how we can resolve these conflicts. In another book, *Insight and Responsibility*, Erik Erikson defines the golden rule in a brilliant and fundamental way that I've not heard mentioned in any discussion so far either here or in the United Nations. It states that I do for you what strengthens you simultaneously as it strengthens me, given my age, stage, development, and position, and your age, stage, development, and position—which makes ethics relative.

Juergensmeyer: Thank you for those references.

Dr. Gurcharan Singh [of Marymount College]: I'm neither a student nor a teacher of religion, but I've a great interest in it, and each one of the presentations this morning has been a great learning experience for me. I would like to emphasize what Professor Thurman said: what we learn to think of religion from those who occupy the positions of power distorts religion to an extent. Therefore, he tried to draw our attention to the essence of what the prophet said and the basis for commonality there. With regard to one observation made by Professor Henkin—that religion isn't about rights, but about duties—let me point out that five hundred years ago Guru Nanak said that denial of the rights of other people, disrespect for their identity, is very bad. He talked about not only my rights but everybody's rights. If you deny them, it is like violating your very own fundamental taboos. We all thought God was a male chauvinist, but Guru Nanak addresses God as my father and my mother, as my best friend. Friend can be male or female, even a gay person. He said, you are my best friend and you are my best guide in this world and you are my protector. Now in all of this he broke the barrier, which I think was radical.

What I want to say is that I think there is a great deal of commonality if we go beyond those people who speak in the name of the religion and who distort the religion. To borrow Professor Thurman's terms, the liberal, the democrat, the secularist, and the capitalist may think that only they know about human rights. But I think we can build a bridge by way of religion. I believe every religion talks about kindness, about compassion, about sharing, about truth, and about justice. All we have to do is to explore these more fully and try to understand how we can find a common ground.

[Unidentified]: I believe that most of the world religions do define the rights of people, but they define them in the context of rights that are necessary to fulfill an obligation to whatever god is present in that religion. What we should address is how we can redefine or find a new emphasis within our own traditions of obligation that could be extended toward a universal conception of human rights.

Prof. Richard Falk: Let me just make a short comment about the idea that the way to approach this issue is by way of a minimalist shared content. I think that's unexceptionable and very helpful in counteracting some rhetorical excesses that one finds in some of the documents that are before us. But I think one mustn't overlook the difficulty about what that minimum is. I don't think one can escape the problem by putting it in very abstract terms. For instance, when I stress the importance of the economic and social realities of the peoples of the world, for that to be meaningful I must confront some difficult and very contested issues. In other words, saying it's minimal doesn't really overcome the task of creating a meaningful existential foundation for a global ethic, one that can work for the peoples of the world and that relates to life. One still has a lot of work to do even along the lines that Sissela proposed. Let's not be distracted by the diversities of maximalist conceptions.

[Unidentified]: This is a provocative issue, one I think we have to contend with. What are the ontological foundations of our values? Do they come from something that can be measured, or from our intellectual deliberations? All of the religious traditions suggest that values come from some kind of immeasurable ultimate source. Whether it's called god or whether it's called the void, it is something more primordial than what the intellect offers. But even if the religious traditions attempt to articulate what is revealed of that immeasurability, that mystery, they are not in and of themselves that mystery. So I think we should make a distinction between the source of the revelation in each religion and its articulation. Otherwise we end up in a morass, trying to analyze which ritual, which expression is consistent with our own culturally determined world view.

The other point is that recognition of the mystery gives rise to a quality that does not exist at all in secular humanism—humility, a sense of humility concerning the human endeavor. With it comes the awareness that we may not be here for the purpose of conquering and running the world, and that the UN and all such human institutions may only be the second team. We may not be here for the purpose of being in charge, but to learn more about this mystery. Religions, because they're institutions, have a tendency to forget this sense of human limitation and often claim the superiority of their expression. So unless we—as thinkers and reflectors on these transcendent ethical issues—are willing to collectively move beyond the intellect, acknowledge our limitations, and hold religions to a certain standard of humility, reminding them that there is something beyond them to which they are subject, we will remain in the realm of the aesthetics of intellectual discourse when we should be tapping into the power of that immeasurability.

Fr. Luis Dolan: Personal experience leads me to worry about something, and I'd like to put it forth as a question. When Hans Küng wanted to present his global ethic, I put him in touch with people at the UN. One of the critical points that came up then and that continues to come up is how very Western his approach is. Like all such work in universities in the West, his is excessively "sanitized." Whereas people from the East come to Columbia or Harvard to get their PhDs, or to Oxford or wherever, few Westerners do it the other way around. We're just starting to move in that direction due to the importance of some Eastern religious traditions. Another aspect of this issue is that the rules of ethics are usually produced by victors. The United Nations Declaration is an instance of human rights proclaimed by a group of victors. The poor people who lost had nothing to say. After the Gulf War, too, conditions were defined by the victors alone. But some of the founders of religions were losers, starting with the founder of mine, the person I believe in with all my heart, Jesus Christ.

So my question to the panelists is this: To what degree can common people and common groups influence your personal thinking?

Lois Kellerman: I'm an ethical culture leader, a secular religious humanist, and a bit of an oxymoron. I have two follow-up comments. The first is that I loved the distinction between the minimalist and maximalist. I think it's a wonderful strategy, and I think we do need to begin and try to develop a minimum. But if this means mere consensus, we have to ask ourselves a very hard question. If the minimalist perspective is not enough to sustain a liveliness toward a future, if it leads to human suicide for example, would we be willing to settle for that at the minimum? In what way are we the yeast in this, in what way do we want to up the ante on the minimum in order to make it adequate for survival—spiritually and physically?

Second, I thought that question about the woman thrown on the pyre was very revealing, because I know people who would do it. And I think it was revealing that you had far more consensus among you than you thought. Your strategies are different—universalist, more Western, or comparativist—but in fact your longings are the same. Your longings are for union, for harmony, for community. But I'm not sure that those are everyone's longings. In fact, the world seems to have a very dark shadow. How are we going to begin the dialogue with that shadow of ourselves?

Catholicism makes a very interesting distinction between optimism and hope: optimism is not something that we should look for often, but hope is always possible and must be possible. So I'm looking to move beyond a facile and surface optimism to a deeper hopefulness that comes out of dialogue. But there are people who love blood. It's only recently, in the last five thousand years or so, that religion has gone ethical. In fact, there were twenty or thirty thousand years during which we can intuit that there were other things than ethics at the center. So again, I stand on my commitment. I want to make all religions heed the ethical voice; but we often seem to be apologists, revising history out of a need and longing to use both religious and secular tools to create a more ethics-centered world.

Juergensmeyer: I think that follows up very well on the concerns of Professor Falk. Now, let's ask the panelists to respond.

Bok: I want to say that I found these comments, especially taken together, very rich and fruitful. I'm very grateful, and I have a lot to think about. To begin with Professor Falk, I think you're absolutely right. I didn't mean to say that we should only stick with the minimalist. I think we need to sort out these minimal values and find the ones that can be recognized even by a child or a young person—those that trigger a response when we see the grief of the mother of a disappeared person in Latin America, or when we learn what happened as a result of our war in Vietnam, or the war in Afghanistan, or other wars. We can reach out then. We don't need to know very much to understand what has gone on.

At the same time, it's absolutely true that this would never be enough. On the contrary. We have to use that effort to reach out to find a common beginning point. At the same time we need people who say, as you did, Professor Falk, that there isn't enough in the Universal Declaration. We also need the maximalist approaches. Some will say one thing, others, coming from a religious perspective, will say a different thing. We need that debate among the different maximalist views at the same time we have the debate between the minimalist and the maximalist. What I criticized about the various documents was their failure to separate these positions. Everything was thrown in a jumble, so we all feel a little uncomfortable because we know we can't go along with everything that's there. At the same time, we're not sure where the dividing lines are.

To the person who asked what actually is common, I would say there are many things that are common among societies. For example, slavery and oppression of women. But being common is obviously not enough. Not all societies have had slavery, not all societies have had oppression of women. I'm talking about what's absolutely necessary in any society for it to survive. And what is necessary is, for instance, that there be no indiscriminate killing within the group. Yes, some people within the group may, unfortunately, be killed, but there must be some boundaries. As soon as you set some boundaries, you've got a little corner from which to argue outwards and ask, "Why do you think you can kill people of such and such a race; why do you think you can oppress people of such and such a gender?"

Finally, I also want to comment on the very interesting statement about the ontological origins of values. That came from the maximalist camp, and it's extremely important. Some people say that values originate with a particular god, some people say they are to be found in nature. Cicero said they were inscribed in our minds. Others say that they are constructed, that as communities settle down and develop, they have to construct something. There are many different views as to these origins, and I find them all fascinating. I don't think we need to resolve this disagreement at all. It's a maximalist disagreement, but we would be very much the poorer without it and its like.

With respect to humility, I think it is probably the most important human virtue. It is one that will grow as we encounter other cultural traditions, other ways of looking at things. I would only disagree with the claim that humility has not been stressed in secular traditions. Perhaps the greatest secular moralist, Kant, was of extreme humility. Henry Sedgwick, a utilitarian, was a very humble person who also stressed humility. I don't think that any religion or all religions have a monopoly on it.

And just one comment to the priest who spoke. I was so glad that he brought up the question of how we begin to exercise whatever values we regard as most fundamental in our own lives. Gandhi and a number of other leaders have shown that what you claim—whether for the universe as a whole, or the United Nations, or any other group—will matter only if you try to take it seriously in your own life.

Thurman: First, to Professor Falk. I feel compelled, since my wife is not here, to say that socialism is not dead. It's still alive in Sweden. Scandinavian socialism, which has never gone in the Russian or the Chinese direction and has created a very wonderful society, has produced wonderful people like Professor Bok and exported them all over the world. But it's never appreciated by Americans, who always pretend that it's inconsiderable because it's such a small place. But it's as big as New York City! There's plenty of babysitting and quite a sensible society. I do agree with you, though, that with the supposed death of the Cold War and the supposed triumph of capitalism, all bets are off, and the polarization in this country between the rich and the poor is growing in an alarming way. We see how the Congress has got a stranglehold on every positive movement. I completely agree with that.

Similarly in the case of the religions there is a danger. We have to remember that at the time of the Universal Declaration of Human

Rights, a common assumption on the part of secular intellectuals (who were the main ones behind it) was that religions were inevitably disappearing in the world. What was predicted was a withering away not of the state but of religions. The subsequent fifty years have proved that to be absolutely wrong, although until the unraveling of the Russian empire it wasn't as clear cut as it has been in the last five years. But then there is a danger that religions, now encouraged that they withstood the onslaught of secularism in its extreme form of communism, and in its less extreme form of secularism in the capitalist world, may now take up their old bad habits of triumphalism and insist on having more children so their populations will increase, and so on. This kind of negative thing is incredibly destructive to the planet.

The process of beginning to try to mobilize the religions in a pluralistic context to do this job is very, very important. It may finally be possible that scholars of religion and people concerned with religion may come out of being considered utter marginalities, which is what we have been in the past in the Western academy, for example.

My second point has to do with Dr. Bok's paper. She strongly urged the maximalist approach as much as people could do in their own free time, so to speak, but to try to create a minimalist basis for a boundary of agreement. She was not slighting the benefit of maximalism, in other words. This comes through clearly when you read her paper.

Third, I think that was an excellent comment the gentleman made about the ultimate source. The secular humanists also have an ultimate source. They don't like to refer to it as that, but their notion of science as discovering the nature of reality, coming from nature, may also be referred to as an ultimate source. Everyone has some such notion of an ultimate source.

Everyone also has a caveat within their tradition, what I call an "idolatry caveat." Of course the Buddhist and Confucian traditions are a little less hung up on it because they don't believe in an all-powerful gentleman sitting up there controlling everything. But still, they have this caveat that finally, whatever human beings think, even the so-called formulations of the revelations they received involved the human hand and the human mind, and therefore are limited. Anyone who would put such a formulation above an individual human life is in some sense an idolater, a conceptual idolater. Luckily, the secular humanist scientists have finally come to realize that they don't know the nature of reality, and they finally admit it. Of course, they're still pretending that they're going to catch all the neurons in the brain, or they're going to catch every atom in that subway under Texas if they could just build it, but basically they've admitted that they do not know the nature of reality and that there's always more to be discovered no matter how much you discover.

So we can refer to an ultimacy of reality that will cause people's arrogance to back away, and we must do that with religions. For example, I have a friend who is a Muslim, and we were in those dialogues that Mark [Juergensmeyer] referred to. I used to love to kid this friend a little because he is a wonderful, urbane, intelligent man, but now and then he would get a little heated up in discussion. At one point, he slammed his fist on a table and said, "God said his last word in the Koran, and he won't speak again." I said, "Well, my friend, how many languages do you speak?" "Oh, six or seven," he said. And I said, "God is tired of language learning?" After a moment of contemplating a cavalry charge, he laughed, and we had some ease in the moment. In other words, who is to say what the ultimate source can do again in the future? Why should we want to limit a particular revelation? If God is all-capable and all-creative, then we can't say what is going to happen. But this is the level at which religious people need to be challenged, to remember other aspects of their own traditions where there may be "loopholes" or something like that.

Finally, I agree with Father Dolan's comment that this sort of thing must take its cue from the common people. What I want to say is something that I've come to feel more and more because of my work in the last years on the Tibetan situation. Genocide is still taking place there unabated, and still backs are turned to it by everyone in the world. Still there is silence on it in all official circles because it's an embarrassment to business. Because of this, I have come to the conclusion that the concept of sovereignty is a very destructive one to human rights nowadays.

In the old days of imperialism, the notion of sovereignty was of a bunch of kings having a little war for amusement on the Polish border or somewhere in between their hunting seasons. And this idea of sovereignty is used by extremely pernicious governments to pretend that individual human beings under their control, maybe by invasion or by accident, are completely unable to be protected by the other people in the world. This is indeed the single concept that prevents those who think in terms of global institutions from really helping out in cases of individual need that exists in various countries around the world. We call it the United Nations, but if we thought of the peoples of the world as the United Peoples, as the indigenous people in their movement have reminded us, there might be as much as a fifth of the world's population who do not feel represented by the national governments that monopolize the dialogue and debate in the United Nations.

In the last fifty years, fortunately, the United Nations has moved from fifty to a hundred and eighty or so members. But obviously it will have to move further. The three Baltic states which were once under the control of an invisible imperial power are now members of the UN, and there should be many more small states enjoying this dialogue. But we'll never get to that point until we mobilize global ethics and the power of the world religions to challenge this sacrosanct and, I think, highly obfuscatory notion of sovereignty, which is used by illegitimate governments as a way of bludgeoning defenseless individuals.

Juergensmeyer: I might give a somewhat different response to Professor Falk than Professor Thurman gave with regard to the moral challenge arising from the collapse of Communism. I would suggest that it may be the politicization of religion that increasingly will provide this challenge throughout the world, as the title of my book, *The New Cold War?*, implies. In some ways, religious nationalism has become the new ideological challenge to libertarian, democratic capitalism as we know it in the West. It challenges not only in the negative way that we've frequently seen, but also in a positive way, by stating its own moral virtues and its own basis for a moral order founded not just on reason, but on ethical sentiments that all people can share.

But there is not going to be an easy outcome to this confrontation. I think Professor Falk and the last speaker are absolutely right about the difficulties of forging even a minimal consensus. In the last chapter of my book, I puzzle over precisely this problem with regard to religious nationalists. After talking with many fundamentalists throughout the world, especially in the Middle East and South Asia and Central Asia, I have arrived at a kind of desperation about whether any simple compromise can be reached.

I would suggest that there are really three categories of value. There are things that we can consent to relatively easily—the value of life, the dignity of all persons. There are things that we might grudgingly consent to, such as the value of collective entities as arbiters of moral truth. And then there are things that "we" as the products of the enlightened ideologies of the West will never consent to or feel comfortable with. One of these is the notion that a collective judgment about value takes precedence over individual rights. Take the Salman Rushdie case. Most Muslims, regardless of whether they believe a price should be put on a person's head—and most do not—nonetheless agree that it was valid and right to censor this person who chose to speak out, to conceive in this way against the virtues of Islam. Most of us will never agree with that. We're going to have to face the sad fact that, at least on some levels, we may never achieve a consensus. We'll have to make do with the things that we can agree on.

I have one last story to tell. In Cairo, I was talking with some fundamentalist supporters of the Muslim brotherhood about the following problem (but not publicly, since they'd be put in jail immediately): how to live with other people. The interesting thing is that we think they don't think about this question, but actually they think about it all the time. They think about exactly the thing we're talking about—how to live with other people in a plural world, where other people's ethics are not the same as theirs. They want to dominate their culture and impose their particular ethical point of view, but they're concerned about what to do with other, minority points of view. One said he had come up with a solution. In his mind—this is my description of his idea—there is a kind of split-level Shar'iah. He said, of course there should be a Shar'iah. Everybody who is in Egypt should obey the Shar'iah, the law that we all agree on. He gave himself as an example. He went to Columbia University, and while he was in New York, he obeyed all the laws of city. He stopped at a red light; he went on the green. He was very careful not to spit on the pavement. He did all of the things that are required within this civil society in order to get along with other people. When he got home, he and his family were good Muslims. He wouldn't attack the corner liquor store because, according to the Shar'iah of this area, you can have liquor stores on the corner, but his family wouldn't have any.

To his mind, there could be a split-level Shar'iah. You could have the Shar'iah, a common law for everybody, but there would also be a special one just for people of a particular faith. I said, "Ah, this is very interesting. This means that you could conceive of a kind of a general values for Egyptian society that would apply to Coptic Christians—the minority with the most problems there—as well as to Muslims, and that the Coptic Christians would agree with because of their own tradition." He agreed to this, so I added, "You would let them drink, and you would let them do other things that Christians do because they're Christians." Again, he said, yes. I said, "Well, this is terrific. By extension, you could apply the same logic to secularists, people who have been Muslims but have been convinced by whatever enlightened virtues or secular ideas that they should be part of a different community and a different standard of faith. They, too, should be allowed a place where they can drink and go to dirty movies, or do whatever secular Muslims do if they're secular." He thought about this, and said, "No. That's going a little bit too far."

So consensus is going to be difficult. There are always going to be things that we can't agree on. We may have to face the awful possibility that we're simply going to have to live, as we did during the old Cold War, with the idea that there are values and organizations that are different from ours. We can agree on some things, but eventually we may simply have to come to a kind of moral entente. For the sake of life on this planet, we may simply have to accept the fact that some people inevitably and ultimately are going to be different.

Panel #3

• • •

THE WORLD'S RELIGIONS: PROSPECTS FOR A GLOBAL ETHIC IN SUPPORT OF HUMAN RIGHTS

• • •

Fr. Luis Dolan (Moderator)
United Nations Representative, Temple of Understanding

Peter Awn
Department of Religion, Columbia University

Rebequa Getahoun Murphy
United Nations Representative, Baha'is of the US

Sallie B. King
Department of Philosophy and Religion, James Madison University

Panel #3 Opening Remarks by

FR. LUIS DOLAN (Moderator)

• • •

Fr. Luis M. Dolan, C.P., director of International Programs and representa-
tive at the United Nations for the Temple of Understanding, is a native of
Argentina. As a Catholic priest and member of the Passionist congregation,
Fr. Dolan has worked extensively with NGOs and as a consultant to
UNESCO on the proposed UN Year on Tolerance. He also works closely
with UNDP and UNICEF.

I think we all agree that inter-religious dialogue and cooperation is an essential element for the future of the world. If we are unable to create it, the end of the world, the apocalypse, may be nearer than we imagine. We might keep this in mind this afternoon as we move on from our discussion of a global ethic to concentrate on the topic of religions and human rights. You're going to hear three excellent papers from three different religious perspectives—Islamic, Buddhist, and Baha'i. As for our topic itself, those of you who are in contact with the UN know that not all countries accept the term "human rights." It's not part of their mentality, so its links to religion remain tenuous.

"Right" is a legal term, not an ethical concept in many countries. In the UN this is a very serious concern, as it is in the international community itself. In 1981, a document was approved, *The Universal Declaration on Religious Freedom and Belief.* It was not an easy document to create, but once it was approved, we had an academic, legal, and global paper to start working on. There are a number of us who are working with it now, trying to see whether it's time to move on to a convention. There is also an agency of the UN, UNITAR, that has expressed increasing interest in the issues of religion and spirituality. We also see that in the upcoming world conferences, particularly in the proposed plan of action for the World Summit on Social Development, there is overt mention of the importance of values and the importance of spirituality. Then, of course, there are the NGOs, many of which are represented here today.

There is also a group of inter-religious bodies working with the International Association for Religious Freedom that always has something on this topic at their conferences. Their present secretary-general has written a well-known book on the issue of human rights and religion. It is also one of the main concerns of the World Conference on Religion and Peace (WCRP), probably the largest of all inter-religious groups. And everyone knows the extraordinary work that Marcus Braybrooke and the World Fellowship of Religions have done. Then there is the group I represent, the Temple of Understanding. A couple of months ago I met Ambassador Somavia, the head of the government committee for the World Summit. He asked me to try to gather people of different religions from different parts of the world to prepare a paper on spiritual values and the UN to use as a background for UN documents.

Finally, I would say that the topic of spirituality and development has been a basic one for anybody who believes in the international community. We started from an economic approach to development, and we made some progress, then we went to a macro-economic approach—we had human development reports, the UN Development Programme—and now, today, we're beginning to ask that difficult question: how do we enter the realm of values?

Panel #3 Presentation by

PETER AWN

• • •

*Peter J. Awn is Professor of Religion at Colum-
bia University where he has taught since
receiving his PhD from Harvard in 1978. His
publications include* Satan's Tragedy *and*
Redemption: Iblis in Sufi Psychology, *for
which he was awarded the ACLS Committee on
History of Religions book prize. Professor Awn
was recipient of a National Endowment for the
Humanities grant to conduct a project on* The
Islamic Vision of Religion and Literature: Four
Classical Texts.

Most current discussions of Islam have
an underlying political agenda, one
that often distorts Muslim attitudes towards human rights and their potential for a global ethic. It seems too easy these days to carica-
ture the Islamic world as fundamentalist, anti-
democratic, and anti-human rights. For those of
us who study Islamic religion and the history of
Islamic societies, what is overwhelming is the extraordinary diversity that has pervaded Islamic
history. Islam, which spread to Europe and
through Asia and Africa, has now taken root in all
the major cultures of the world. And it has added
great ethical values as well as cultural values as it
has spread. Most important for those of us who
study Islamic religion is its extraordinary intellectual richness—the ability of Islamic societies in the
medieval and modern periods to engage in internal debate about significant ethical questions.

There is no doubt that you will find in Islamic

> "One cannot
> avoid the fact
> that embedded
> in many religious
> traditions is an
> affirmation that,
> given the proper
> context, aggres-
> sive behavior is
> not only permit-
> ted, but morally
> sanctioned."

societies—as you do in Christian societies, Jewish societies, and others—conservative elements that claim to represent the truth of the faith. When those claims to truth cut off dialogue, they in many ways represent an isolationist stance. But if one were to regard that as the key that unlocks the truth of Islam, one would be misguided and would clearly not be taking into account Islamic history in its richness. Islam is a populist faith, open to all races and classes, and not in any way restrictive in terms of gender as far as access to ultimate truth and salvation are concerned. Its consistent reverence for human beings is clearly embedded in the Koran itself, which tells us that God created all humans by breathing into them his very own spirit. That is what distinguishes us from all other aspects of creation: to literally possess within ourselves the spirit of God. Again in the Koran, there is a constantly reiterated concern for those most vulnerable within society—for the poor, for widows, for orphans, for those who normally fall through the cracks. The responsibility for those human beings falls upon the community itself.

The intellectual world of Islam has in very important periods represented an authentic space for interreligious and intellectual dialogue. Clearly in medieval Muslim Spain there was a time of extraordinary, rich interaction among Christians, Jews, and Muslims. The same can be said of Fatimid Egypt, and of Ottoman Turkey in the sixteenth century. These were times when Islam was a catalyst for intellectual development and equally important for its willingness to foster intercommunal exchange. We don't often look to the mystical tradition of Islam as an important factor in understanding the cultural and religious richness of the Islamic community, but mysticism has been one of the most important shaping elements in the Islamic world from the early medieval period down to the modern day.

Let me just illustrate one aspect of mysticism that I find particularly important for our discussions today. Oftentimes it is the mystics who have challenged isolationist and rigid understandings of the place of law and institution within a religious structure. They have insisted that there is an experience of God that takes us beyond the limits of our own society, beyond the limits of our own religious law, and beyond the limits of our own institutional religious structures. This is a broader religious experience that is to be discovered within the family of Islam as well as within other religious families. These are different voices, diverse voices, voices within the community that will argue, often in a creative way, about these ideals.

Islam does present universalist truth claims. Not only is it a populist religion, it sees its goal as universal: all the world will eventually embrace the faith of Islam. Clearly, therefore, questions have to be asked within the community as to how such a universalist perspective can allow one to fully acknowledge the rights of others outside of the community. This is a serious question and one that should not be shirked by the community itself.

Another problem arises in communities such as those based in Islam, Judaism and, in certain ways, Christianity. They place an emphasis on divinely revealed religious law as the source of human behavior that will lead to ultimate salvation, and such divinely revealed legal systems do on occasion run counter to some of the ideals articulated in the Global Ethic and in the Declaration of Human Rights. One could say that these legal systems often enshrine a patriarchal structure, which, though it reverences women, often places them in a role different from, and, at times, subservient to that of men. So, do they promote true equal rights, or do they place serious limitations on certain members of the community?

Perhaps most challenging for the Islamic community, and I would say this is true for Christianity and Judaism as well, is the traditional legitimation of aggressive behavior to combat the forces of moral and social evil. When giving lectures on Islam, I've often been asked why it is that Islam is the most violent of the world's religions. My response is: show me a religion that isn't potentially violent. Buddhism? I'll buy you a one-way ticket to Sri Lanka, then tell me what you think. The potential for violence exists within all of the great religious traditions. And I would suggest to you that, from an insider's perspective, acts of aggressive behavior are often understood not as blind aggression but as important moral acts. If one identifies an evil, an evil that threatens the community, then it becomes the moral responsibility of the individual and the group to combat that evil. Of course, the question is, who determines what really represents moral evil and its opposite, moral good? Still, this notion of fighting for moral good is endemic to most major religious traditions.

In the mythology at the heart of a number of religions, especially in the West, we find paradigms for a kind of transformational violence.

It's always interesting to take someone who knows nothing about Christianity or Roman Catholicism into a Roman Catholic church and up to the altar, and, after explaining the sacrifices, to point above the altar and say, "By the way, that dead body hanging on a piece of wood is God." For someone who knows nothing about it, it is a grotesque symbol of violence. A dead man, nailed to a piece of wood with thorns sticking out of his head. What is positive in that? For an insider, this is an extraordinary symbol of victory because of the way that Jesus literally goes through death and is transformed—he offers that to all of his followers. There are mythic parallels in Judaism as well as in Islam. One cannot avoid the fact that embedded in many religious traditions is an affirmation that, given the proper context, aggressive behavior is not only permitted, but morally sanctioned.

For those of us who espouse nonviolence, a great deal of dialogue must take place before certain groups in traditions like Islam, Judaism, and Christianity fully appreciate this ideal. What I want to leave you with is the conviction that Islam has in its past manifested an extraordinary adaptability—a willingness to raise serious questions, to confront serious questions, and, in fact, to offer leadership in terms of serious intellectual and religious dialogue.

Panel #3 Presentation by

REBEQUA GETAHOUN MURPHY

• • •

Rebequa Getahoun Murphy is the representative to the United Nations for the Baha'is of the United States. Educated in Ethiopia, the former Soviet Union, India, and the United States, Ms. Getahoun Murphy has extensive experience in community development work in Africa and has a special interest in issues concerning the UN, women, children, peace, and the environment.

A ny discourse on global ethics from a Baha'i perspective would have to center around a particular passage from our writings that I want to quote. "The well-being of mankind, its peace and security, are unattainable unless and until its unity is firmly established." You see, it isn't just the minimalist goal of mutual toleration that we want; we feel that the future of humanity depends upon our ability to go beyond mere tolerance and really build a world audacious enough to say, "The essential oneness of humanity is what we believe in." We cannot simply be satisfied with a minimalist approach, but we can see that it points forward along the path of human civilization.

This morning as I was listening to one of the talks, I was struck by how very seriously we sometimes take ourselves—sometimes too seriously. The twentieth century is only a momentary stop along the road of an ever-advancing civilization.

"We feel that the future of humanity depends upon our ability to go beyond mere tolerance and really build a world audacious enough to say, 'The essential oneness of humanity is what we believe in.'"

We are not going to define everything about spirituality, about ethics, about anything in the ultimate sense. We believe we are part of an ever-advancing, evolving, changing civilization, but at this point in time we do have certain things going for us in spite of all outward appearances. For example, who would have thought, fifty or sixty years ago, that the Germans and the French would be on the same side? We don't have to go back five or ten thousand years in history. I think the belief that human beings are totally incorrigible—that we'll always be disunified and prone to violence—breeds an international atmosphere which allows us to tolerate the most inhumane treatment of one another. But I don't think we are born with that belief. We are socialized into it. Since the societies we live in today have evolved, they have the ability to evolve further. We can't presume that the entire future of the human race is to be defined by what is on the planet today.

As the fiftieth anniversary of the United Nations approaches, there will be a lot of discussion about what role the religious community has played in the growth, development, and promotion of the United Nations. When you look at the original forty-five or so nongovernmental organizations that were invited to comment on the United Nations Charter prior to its signing, there were few religious organizations involved. As time passed, however, religious NGOs have done an outstanding job of promoting the UN and its charter. In spite of the fact that it was a document written by the victors, it articulated the best that the human spirit longed for after war. Now the challenge remains our ability to implement these values. In this regard, the support of religious communities has become more and more crucial to the United Nations during the past fifty years, particularly in the United States, where support for the UN ebbs and flows.

The vast majority of the peoples of the world don't define their values based on what their governments say. Their values come from deeply held religious beliefs. For this reason, the role of religious NGOs in promoting the interests of the UN among their constituencies is extremely vital. Unfortunately, the whole discourse of the role of religion in governance of human society has been marginalized to the detriment of humanity.

Although religions have a long history of fighting and bickering with each another, they have also had the capacity to uplift the human spirit. A passage from the Baha'i writing reads as follows: "Religion confers upon man eternal life and guides his footsteps in the world of morality. It opens the doors of unending happiness and bestows everlasting honor upon humankind." Religion has been the basis of all civilization and progress, but we have shortchanged humanity during the past hundred years or so. A particularly Western notion about the separation of church and state has compartmentalized different sectors of the human experience. Earlier today someone asked me how we can talk about global ethics without bringing business into it. I agreed that business has to be brought in, but how can we talk about global ethics if we don't bring religion into the discussion? I don't mean just religious leaders but religious individuals at the level of society—the mothers and fathers who instill values in their children—since these children will eventually go out and do good or evil.

A love for all of humanity is a value which can be instilled in children. I'd like to give the example of one of my sons when he was about seven years old. He came home and said to me, "Mom, you know it doesn't bother me when kids call me 'nigger.'" My reaction was to say, "What do you mean it doesn't bother you that they call you 'nigger!'" And he said, "Well, the reason they say it is because they're ignorant. They don't understand that humanity is one." As I said to myself at the time, we do have the power to overcome. We should encourage all voices to be heard, but those of us that truly believe humanity has a glorious future, that we can construct civilizations better than the ones we've had—better in an evolutionary sense, that we can truly become members of one family, cannot allow our views to be shaken by the voices of dissent.

I think we have the power within the religious communities to come together and articulate views which could profoundly change life on the planet. I'm not talking about cosmetic arrangements here. Formulating an ethic that takes into consideration all aspects of human civilization, from the home to international bodies like the United Nations, will require a profound change in the manner in which we view ourselves—a change in the way we relate to each other in our homes, a change in our interactions with our coworkers, in the governments that we bring into being, in the decisions we make in business, in politics, in religion. It will require a profound change, and the realization that first and foremost we are spiritual beings with the ability to rise above the constraints imposed on us by society.

Our vision as Baha'is is that, in the future, we will see all people united as members of one family. This belief is embedded in our moral vocabulary, in our discourse, in our belief system, in the manner in which we educate our children, and in the manner in which we elect our governing bodies at the local, the national, the international level. It is the bedrock on which we found everything we do—the total acceptance of the oneness of the human family. We are serenely confident that this unity will come to pass. However, in the world today, we're like the farmer who has tilled the soil, nurtured the soil, and sown the seed, invites a friend over and says, "Look at my farm," but the friend only sees the soil. But the farmer knows and has absolute faith that some day a crop will grow there, and he or she will be able to harvest it. As Baha'is, we are sometimes like that farmer. We say to people, believe us, you are basically spiritual beings and a global civilization will indeed emerge which, while preserving the rights of individuals, will provide an atmosphere in which all the peoples of the world will be able to nobly play their part in the advancement of humanity.

In conclusion, I would like to offer one more quotation from the Baha'i writings. "The unification of the whole of mankind is the hallmark of the stage which human society is now approaching. Unity of the family, of the tribe, of city-state, nation have been successfully attempted and fully established. The anarchy inherent in state sovereignties is moving towards a climax." That is the stage we're in right now. That's what we see. "A world growing to maturity must abandon selfishness, recognize the oneness and wholeness of the human family, and establish once and for all the machinery that can best incarnate this fundamental principle of its life."

SALLIE B. KING

• • •

Sallie B. King is head of the Department of Philosophy and Religion at James Madison University. Receiving her PhD in religion from Temple University, she has taught courses in Asian religions and in philosophy at a number of universities. She has special interests in the development of Buddhism with expertise in Sino-Japanese Buddhism and the philosophy of religion.

I want to begin by discussing human rights from a Buddhist perspective. We heard this morning that the UN Declaration and the proposed Global Ethic are too Western. I think Buddhism offers some direct responses to these kinds of concerns.

As some of you know, a number of Buddhist scholars and intellectuals have commented negatively about the very idea of human rights. They have based their critique on Buddhist concepts and values, and I sympathize with their concerns. I'm a philosopher myself. The concerns Buddhists have about this idea of human rights can be extracted from the following quotation. In 1956, William Earnest Hocking wrote, "Free individuals, standing for their rights, are 'the best fruit of modernity'."* Now, from a Buddhist perspective,

> "Since all humans are equal in their ability to become a Buddha, Buddhism is committed in principle to human equality, and many Buddhists today are struggling to win that equality."

---

*William Ernest Hocking, *The Coming Civilization*; cited in Leroy S. Rouner, "Introduction," in Leroy S. Rouner, ed., *Human Rights and the World's Religions* (Notre Dame: University of Notre Dame Press, 1988).

there are two problems with this sort of idea. The first is simply the notion of an autonomous individual, some kind of isolated, free-standing island. This idea does not fit in the Buddhist world view. To a Buddhist, Western emphasis on the individual enshrines something that does not exist and will never exist. Moreover, such an idea abets the human tendency towards egomania. Second, the notion of rights also brings with it a larger problem for a Buddhist. Given that, in Buddhism, the most basic reality of life is our mutual interdependence and interconnectedness, it is unnatural and unproductive in the extreme to construct a world view that draws lines between individuals and groups, pitting one against the other. One should expect nothing good or viable to emerge from this kind of construction.

I'll give a brief theoretical response to these problems first and then offer a more practical response. The theoretical response can be summarized as follows: why not think of my "rights" as the other side of the coin of your responsibilities. Buddhists have always been very willing to talk about responsibility—then my right to life would be your responsibility not to kill me. So there should be no reluctance to speak of rights if one is willing to speak of responsibilities. More important, though, there's a response in Buddhist practice that really overshadows any kind of theoretical concern. In the modern world (most of my examples will be of Buddhism in the modern world), it's very significant that the Buddhist leaders who have had extensive dealings with the international community—for example, His Holiness the Dalai Lama and the Vietnamese monk and activist, Thich Nhat Hanh—show no hesitation whatsoever in speaking of human rights. If you read their works or listen to their speeches, you see that they frequently employ this kind of language. They're willing to speak of human rights even though it doesn't really fit with a Buddhist perspective. Buddhists are pragmatic. Buddhists are practical. If it gets the job done, they're quite willing to use it.

More important still is the fact that Buddhist social activists in the modern world are already working for human rights by the millions. I want to give you a very brief and necessarily incomplete survey of some of these activities. In India, millions of Hindu Untouchables have converted en masse to Buddhism, primarily for social and political reasons—to renounce the Hindu caste system and to repudiate the larger social and political system that allows that caste system to continue.

The Buddhism that they are constructing is a social way of life and a political challenge first and a spirituality second, since their main interest is in improving their lives. Buddhist organizations from both the East and the West are working actively to support these peoples in their efforts to overcome their oppression and heal its psychological, economic, social, and spiritual wounds.

In Sri Lanka, the organization Sarvodaya Sramadana has engaged vast numbers of monks and lay persons in a development scheme based upon Buddhist principles. They work to develop villages throughout the island on a Buddhist model conceived as an alternative to the model provided by Western capitalism. These efforts have been very successful. These same people have also been working diligently and at great personal risk to resolve the conflict between the Tamils and the Sinhalese. In that, they've been somewhat less successful.

In Thailand, there is a Buddhist social activist named Sulak Sivaraksa. He has stimulated the development of countless NGOs and publications. He has also organized something called the International Network of Engaged Buddhists. "Engaged Buddhism," by the way, means socially and politically engaged Buddhism. This is a massive and very powerful movement in Asia and also in the West. Unfortunately, because of his speeches critical of the government, Sulak is currently standing trial for treason.*

In Burma in 1988, as you probably recall, Buddhist monks and students filled the streets calling for democracy and an end to the repressive rule of the military. Their leader, Aung San Suu Kyi, is motivated by Buddhist principles and a sense of duty to the people. She has spent the years since then under house arrest rather than abandon the cause.

The Tibetan situation you are probably familiar with. His Holiness the Dalai Lama has led the Tibetan liberation movement in a tireless effort to gain the freedom of the Tibetan people. He has done so in a nonviolent manner and against seemingly hopeless odds.

In Vietnam, during the war, Buddhist monks, nuns, and lay people filled the streets to gain the freedom to practice their religion. Ultimately they brought down the Diem regime. In subsequent years, as the war ground on and on, they undertook every nonviolent act conceivable to try to bring the war to an end and to protect the Vietnamese

---

*The judge ultimately ruled that the government failed to provide sufficient evidence that Sulak had committed treason, and the case was thrown out.

people. Because of their efforts, like the Tibetans, they were sent to prison, suffered torture and even death.

In Japan and elsewhere, many millions have joined the Soka Gakkai, one of our sponsors today, a lay Buddhist organization which works through education, dialogue, and cultural exchange to put an end to the constant threat of war, to build international and interreligious understanding, and to protect the environment.

In the West, not surprisingly, Buddhists work on many fronts and in many different organizations. They undertake all kinds of activities—working with AIDS patients, the homeless, the dying, on environmental projects, and in many other areas as well.

The picture would not be complete without mentioning the Buddhist nuns in both the East and West who have organized themselves to overcome millennia of institutional sexism on the part of Buddhism itself. They are actively supported in these efforts by the more progressive wing of Buddhism.

If you look at these examples, and it's an incomplete list, we're talking about millions of people working at the grassroots level, often with charismatic leadership, to be sure, but certainly inspired by their own Buddhist principles. All of these actions, with the possible exception of protecting animals and the environment, fall within the purview of the human rights agenda. They're all working for what we would call freedom of religion, for human equality, for politically open societies, for minimum economic justice, and the like. Millions upon millions of Buddhists have devoted themselves to these efforts, always nonviolently, and often at the risk of their lives. After turning a historic corner, this is the face of Buddhism today. It is a force with a proven ability to inspire millions to risk everything in nonviolent efforts to gain human rights. So Buddhists are squarely in the human rights camp.

The second part of my talk has to do with the Parliament's declaration of a global ethic. I want to construct a Buddhist proposal for a global ethic. As you'll see, the principles that derive from a Buddhist perspective correspond strikingly with the core principles in the handout you received of the Parliament's declaration. To formulate a Buddhist proposal towards a global ethic, the natural starting place is the five lay precepts that constitute a minimum ethical standard for all Buddhists throughout time. The five precepts have always been understood as the minimum one must accept and work with as a Bud-

dhist. They are as follows: no killing, no stealing, no sexual miscon-
duct, no lying, and no taking of intoxicants. For present purposes I will
say no more about the fifth precept—no taking of intoxicants. Unless
you stretch it very far that's primarily an individual ethic, not a social
ethic. The other four, however, have implications that bear on our topic.
Indeed, their ramifications for social ethics have already been discussed
by Buddhist social activists such as Thich Nhat Hanh and Sulak
Sivaraksa.

The first principle that emerges from the Buddhist precepts is a
principle of *nonviolence toward humans and the biosphere*. The first Buddhist precept urges us to avoid all violent behavior and all actions harmful to sentient beings, and more broadly to all living things and to life
itself. You can compare that to the first principle, the first irrevocable
directive, in the Parliament's declaration.

Here I must say a few words on the application of this principle in
the non-human world, since a question that constantly comes up is
about non-human entities. Buddhism sees humans as part of a larger
category called sentient beings, beings with awareness. Thus, Buddhist
nonviolence or non-harmfulness necessarily extends beyond human
beings to all other sentient creatures. But this idea must be balanced
against another. Buddhists have always also understood human beings to be a unique class insofar as they are in a position to take hold of
their destiny, examine their condition, and strive to free themselves
from ignorance. In short, only humans can practice Buddhism and attain enlightenment. To be born human was, from the beginning, regarded as a precious and rare opportunity. Later forms of Buddhism
developed this notion further, concluding that every human being without exception has the capacity to attain Buddhahood and is, at any
given moment, a Buddha-in-the-making.

From a moral perspective, one can draw the following corollaries:
every human being is an incipient Buddha possessing inherent and
immeasurable value, and thus, every human should be protected and
treated in such a way that her or his incipient Buddhahood may be
nurtured. Therefore, the human focus of a human rights agenda is
highly appropriate. At the same time, to bring us back to my starting
point, we must remember that Buddhists believe the principle of non-
harmfulness to humans cannot be separated from a principle of non-
harmfulness to animals, and, indeed, from an attitude of non-harmful-

ness in general based on respect and appreciation for all life forms and for life itself.

Because of this larger concern, protection of the environment has emerged as a prominent component of social activism for Buddhist individuals and groups such as the Dalai Lama, Sulak Sivaraksa, the Sarvodaya Sramadana, the Soka Gakkai, and Thich Nhat Hanh. So in the context of the human rights agenda, Buddhists have long-standing and very important reasons for regarding humans as especially valuable. But in the context of a global ethic, I believe that Buddhists would need to see the principle of nonviolence clearly applied, not only to humans, but also to the planet which sustains all life as we know it.

A second principle that can be derived from a Buddhist perspective for a global ethic is that of *economic justice*. This would correspond, more or less, to the second principle proposed in the World Parliament's declaration. The second Buddhist precept prohibits stealing. Originally, of course, this was a personal ethic: "I will not steal." But contemporary Buddhist activists have expanded its meaning in such a way that it also addresses the theft that one group, society, or nation might practice against another. Traditionally, of course, individual theft was censured because it caused suffering, and Buddhism is all about eliminating the causes of and healing suffering. That is why it takes little effort to enlarge the traditional understanding into a modern realization that the theft practiced by a powerful group or society against a less powerful group or society causes massive suffering and is, thus, antithetical to the most basic of Buddhist principles.

Some rough equity in sharing the world's resources is a necessary corollary for the following reasons. First, people must have enough and ought not suffer because of vast inequities. Buddhism has turned away from asceticism and espouses the Middle Path between luxury and need. All people must have enough for health and well-being in order to support their efforts to fulfill higher needs. Second, vast inequity fuels resentment, anger, and, ultimately, violence. In order to prevent violence, people must have enough, and there must be rough equity between different groups.

This morning Sissela Bok said that economic justice is not part of a minimalist ethic. I think she's wrong. I would say that economic justice derives from a minimalist sense of justice. We have all had the kind of gut reaction that she talked about. Everyone feels immediately that it is not right for some to feast while many starve. We all know this isn't fair. And if we think about our response for even a moment, we can see how it fits into a minimalist sense of justice.

Of course, most societies have had practices that embody this attitude. For example, in traditional societies you don't eat in front of someone who is not eating. Such societies have rules about hospitality and about sharing with someone who is right in front of you. Today, because of modern communications, we are all present in each other's homes. We all sit down to one big meal; only some of us have food on our plates and others of us do not. It is important to realize that economic justice is not only part of a minimalist sense of justice, but also essential to a global ethic if that ethic is to have any relevance for most people on the planet.

The third principle that comes from Buddhist precepts and that could be proposed here encompasses *human rights and human equality.* This principle corresponds to the fourth point in the Parliament's declaration. I've already discussed human rights from a Buddhist perspective; I won't say more except to point out that they belong here as an essential component of a Buddhist proposal for a global ethic. Since all humans are equal in their ability to become a Buddha, Buddhism is committed in principle to human equality, and many Buddhists today are struggling to win that equality.

Let me add a word regarding equality of the sexes in Buddhism. The third Buddhist precept calls for responsible sexual behavior. Contemporary Buddhist social activists have expanded this personal ethic to include injunctions that would eliminate social institutions that trap women in second class status and permit inhumane treatment of women. As I've indicated, Buddhist institutions themselves have been part of this problem; they continue to be part of the problem in some parts of the world. However, Buddhism also has resources for overcoming this problem. The Buddha made it clear that women are as spiritually capable as men. He established orders for nuns and laywomen in order to give them support in the development of their potential. He also included guidelines that would grant nuns protection from demands that might be made of them by monks. There was, for example, an injunction against sewing for monks. Throughout Buddhist history, Buddhist nunneries have often been the only place of refuge for women attempting to escape intolerable conditions in the secular world. I believe that Buddhism today, despite its shortcomings in this regard, favors protecting women, respecting women as men's spiritual equals, and developing women's potential through nurturing social and economic conditions.

The fourth and last principle from a Buddhist perspective involves *truth and the free flow of information*. This would correspond to the third item in the World Parliament's declaration. The fourth precept calls for truthful language. In the Noble Eightfold Path, which further spells out Buddhist behavior, right speech has always been understood to mean language that is constructive, healing, and conducive to social harmony. First and foremost within this category comes freedom of religion. Buddhism was born and developed in a society in which religions and philosophies freely and publicly debated among themselves. Second, Buddhism has always proclaimed the importance of truthful speech. If governments and other powerful groups and individuals cannot be trusted to speak freely and truthfully about themselves, freedom of the press becomes crucial, and other freedoms as well—freedom of movement, freedom of access to information, freedom of assembly, and freedom of speech. From a Buddhist perspective, truth and the free flow of information are two sides of the same coin. In the long run, the peace and harmony of society depends upon truthful relationships based upon accurate knowledge that is shared among society's members.

To conclude, Buddhism is squarely in the human rights camp. It also strongly supports the effort to define a global ethic. Buddhists would not look to this global ethic for the truth since Buddhists don't expect to find truth in words, but they would see it as a useful tool, an expedient means, something that might teach people that there is some common ground for humankind. Such an ethic might undercut the enmity that we feel, the suspicion and distrust we have of people who are not us, since it suggests that we share something. From the Buddhist point of view, anything that can help reduce suffering helps to fulfill the basic purpose of Buddhism. As such, it will be natural to Buddhists to support it.

OPEN DISCUSSION
Following Panel #3

Alex Wayman [to Professor King]: Sallie, you spoke at length and in a very elegant manner, and those were wonderful sentiments, but were you really representing Buddhism? What kind of Buddhism—early Buddhism, like that sometimes called Hinayana, or the Mahayana Buddhism of China, Tibet, etc.? The problem here is that when the Dalai Lama took his position on nonviolence, it was based upon what we might call Mahayana Buddhism, not necessarily early Buddhism.

Also, at the beginning you claimed that Buddhism does not believe in the individual, but you contradicted yourself later by saying that the individual had to take five vows, not to steal, not to lie, etc. Who takes those vows except an individual? If, in every country, everyone says we can't do anything about government today because governments tell lies, and if various religions, including Buddhism, say the individual must not lie, then everything starts with the individual, doesn't it? The individual is not supposed to tell lies. It is not a question here, as I heard this morning, of "all rights." There are only some rights, there are only some persons, there's only a person, an individual who doesn't lie. And if enough persons didn't lie, governments will be forced not to lie. So the individual can do something, even though at the beginning you said there was no individual.

Dawud Assad: I am the president of the Council of Mosques in the United States. First, I want to congratulate Peter Awn for speaking about Islam. I think he did a very good job, even though he's a Christian. But I also want to say that human rights in Islam actually depends upon the oneness of God. Rights come from God, they are not man-made. The source of human rights is the wisdom and measure of God. The commandments issued by God are the basis for Islamic legislation, and as such should be executed through the force of a Muslim's conscience and obedience to God.

Second, Islam has given executive power to judges to punish those who deny rights to others. This runs counter to today's so-called human rights, since these articles are not buttressed by any legislative power. The human rights that we are discussing now are, therefore, little more than pious recommendations.

As you know from the Koran, the first human rights stem from the verse which says to all human beings—Christians, Muslims, Jews, Buddhists, blacks, and whites—We have created you from a man and a woman, and we have made you into tribes and nations. Why? So that you may know one another, not despise each other. The best among you are so not because you are Christian or Muslim or Hindu or American or Palestinian. No, the best one among you is the one who is more fearful of God, who is more conscious of God, who does good for his neighbor, who is more pious. Our Prophet, in his last sermon before passing away, and after he had made a pilgrimage in Mecca, said: All you people, you are from Adam, and Adam is from clay. So there's no difference between a black person and a white, no superiority of black over white, or white over black, except by piety. This is the basis of human rights in Islam.

Another point. Salman Rushdie was mentioned many times this morning, so I hope you will allow me a minute to speak about him. Actually, the issue here is not the right of religious freedom or freedom of expression, but the responsible use of this freedom. I should not stand up now and say, "There is a bomb in this hall. Let's get out." If everybody starts to run, its not a matter of freedom of expression. It's harmful. Muslims wholeheartedly support religious freedom and freedom of expression. But freedom of expression, like all rights, brings responsibility. This applies especially in situations where two rights come into conflict. Very clearly, here, the right of Muslims not to be insulted is in conflict with the right to freedom of expression. This is more of a moral issue than a legal issue. Much of what is in Rushdie's book is prejudiced, monstrous—it is garbage. We are not against freedom of expression, but you have to know how to use it. And you must not insult people because they believe that.

Ann Purvis: I am involved with some of the religious groups at the United Nations Church Center, some of the peace groups and also the ecology groups. I would like to ask the two women speakers about the sources for women's traditions in the world religions. I know that the

Baha'i faith has beautiful texts about the equality and cooperation of the two genders, and I especially have been interested in Tahirih, the female prophetess and teacher. Dr. King, I was interested in your statements about women and Buddhism. What I would like are sources, references to women who have written about Buddhist tradition. Who were these women? Are they leaders today?

Bawa Jain: For the sake of brevity I'll just ask some pointed questions. They're to Professor Peter Awn. One of the things you said is that the Islamic tradition holds that everybody should ultimately embrace Islam. Does that mean Islam advocates intolerance toward other religions? The second part of my question is simply a reply to your statement that every religious tradition has a potential for violence. I don't believe that is true of the Jain religion.

Awn: First, a couple of quick responses to Rebequa Murphy. One, you seemed a little uncomfortable with the separation of church and state, but I would actually argue in favor of it. Imagine Father Dolan doling out highway contracts and things like that. There would be the problem with having a rabbi or a priest or an imam in government. It's not just a matter of protecting people from religious influences in government—I think we're protecting religion from the dirty work of government, from getting sullied by it. In the international sphere, for example, Bawa Jain is forming a caucus on values at the United Nations. I think this should be done from the outside, as an honest broker of sorts. If we arrive at some common ground, that could help inform the discussions of nations while they're still sovereign states.

Then, on the second point. There has been a lot of talk about history being written by the victors and about how values are written by the victors. I think that might have been true before, but in the modern age you find that there's substantial input from academia and elsewhere. You find the losers are writing history more because they have more of an ax to grind. You find that the really liberal people among those who have won can sit back and wonder, "What have I just won? What have I just done?"

When you're on the bottom, or still fighting to regain your old territory or status, you don't tolerate dissent. That's been the argument in the African-American academic community for some time. Still, people felt that there wasn't enough dissent within the community. In Jewish academic history, there was the Israel issue. You didn't have a diversity of opinion in Israel for a long time. And Islam today feels humiliated by the colonial experience. That's why you're seeing a lot of fundamentalism there.

I think that what the prophets who started these religions might have had in common—what makes them prophets and not the typical people who write history books—is that they were losers, as one of our panelists said. They were on the losing end of things, but they went on to create paradigms which were inclusive of the oppressors. Maybe that's a commonality that we can all look towards.

King: First of all, which Buddhism do I represent? I was speaking primarily from the perspective of what's called "engaged Buddhism"— socially and politically engaged Buddhism. I would like to make the point, however, that this is not a small thing. We have a defensive attitude in this country about being "liberal," one that must be put aside when we think about Buddhism. The progressive and liberal people in Buddhism do not have to apologize for themselves. They are influential, and they are guided by some of the most important, most respected leaders in the world. For example, His Holiness the Dalai Lama, Dr. Ariyaratne in Sri Lanka, and Maha Ghosananda in Cambodia. These are people who have the complete love and respect of the people in their countries. They have no need to apologize. These are probably the most important leaders in the Buddhist world. Yes, there is a very conservative wing in Buddhism, but the engaged Buddhist movement crosses the line between Theravada and Mahayana. Two of the figures I mentioned are Theravadans, but they all signed the Global Ethic. They are representative of the most dynamic aspect of Buddhism today.

Now, the second question. I assume most of you are not very interested in the philosophical ins and outs of the Buddhist notion of the individual. So I will only suggest that the place to begin is with the realization that we are not islands. If you look at an individual, you see an entire society reflected within that individual. We are created by our societies as well as our physical environment. That's not to say that human beings are not important and real; they are, as I tried to indicate, extremely important. Human freedom and creativity are extremely important as well. But at the same time, to believe that we're isolated and alone as individuals is, from the Buddhist perspective, an error and a disease of the mind.

In response to the question about sources dealing with distinguished Buddhist women, past and present: Buddhism does have a lot to apologize for in that category. I have myself done research in this area. I've had a difficult time finding sources, and it's not clear whether this is because I am not looking in the right places, or because such women were never there in the first place, or because they were there but nobody ever cared to take note of what they were doing. These kinds of questions can't be answered. There are a few exceptional individuals and a few records that have come down, but it's very, very little compared to what's been preserved for men.

Murphy: First, I'd like to talk about the question of the separation of church and state. I think the world today offers a number of extremes, one of which is for religion to be kept out of most parts of life beyond churches, synagogues, and other places of worship. This is the case in schools in the United States. You can bring up all kinds of things in those schools, but not religion. But when you think about the human beings, it's totally senseless to keep religion out, since one of the most important parts of being human is your belief system. The other extreme is one in which, as Peter Awn suggested, religion is involved in doling out contracts.

But religion can't stand outside, informing the discourse from the sidelines. It has to be an integral part of things. We have to be able to look at physical, social, political, and spiritual being as a whole. There is no reason at all for religion to be an outside force, waiting for the UN to ask it for a comment here and there: "Can we use the term 'spirituality'? Is that okay? Can we use 'God'?" I think we've gotten beyond that. We have to be able to look at all sectors of human existence and deal with the whole being. How we do this is quite negotiable.

The other question has to do with women. I think as far as human rights is concerned, this is probably one of the toughest issues for most religions. In the case of the Baha'i faith, because most Baha'is in the world are first generation and were not raised with the Baha'i teachings, our biggest challenge is to move away from our earlier socialization and really accept what the faith teaches. It is very explicit about the role of women in society, about their rights and prerogatives, and we have materials, compilations from Baha'i writings and other articles that deal with this issue.

Awn: I think your question about universalism and tolerance is a very good one. I think the Islamic belief that Islam should spread throughout the world is very similar to what you find in Christianity—a universalist vision. Intending no disrespect for either tradition, I must say I find the study of religion most interesting at times when it doesn't appear terribly logical. You have an ideal, but what is more interesting is how operative the ideal is at any particular point in history. How concerned are people with promoting that particular value at any particular point in time?

The fact is that it will always be an ideal in Islam, just as it will always be an ideal in certain Christian sectarian movements. But I think greater values, namely pluralism, cultural interaction, and harmony among various groups, are really what motivate most Islamic societies. While it is true that there is proselytizing in certain parts of the Islamic world, it is not a major component of most Islamic societies. So I can understand an outsider asking, "What does this mean? The only way these people will deal with me is if I become them." This may make the outsider feel somewhat threatened. But if you understand how these ideals operate, you find that in fact they aren't the primary motivating force. In the modern period the ideals of pluralism and harmony among groups have clearly taken precedence over them.

I won't go near the second question. Professor Cort, have there ever been Jain rulers who were not terribly nice?

Cort: No, they were always totally benevolent.

Awn: All right. We'll see about that. Just a final response regarding the frequent and very unfortunate use of the Rushdie affair in the press and elsewhere as a kind of final revelation of what Islam is really about. I was at a conference in England run by a very prominent foundation whose main purpose was in fact to ask whether the Rushdie affair proves that Muslim minorities in Europe are by definition anti-democratic. Do they represent a fifth column within democratic societies throughout the world, one that will eventually lead to the destruction of democratic principles? It sounded like what people used to say about

Roman Catholics in the 1920s and '30s in the United States, that there is this person outside society who can reach in and tell you what to do.

In fact, the terrible fear that the Pope would run every Catholic politician's life has now been transferred to the Muslim community. I would say from my perspective, from an outsider's perspective, that I have no problem at all with someone in a religious community saying, "I am wildly offended by what you say. I think what you write and say is garbage." What I find problematic is a religious institution or group having access to the structures of the state, thus allowing it to impose sanctions on people they don't like. That to me is where I would truly find a problem, and it's on that point that I would disagree with the previous speaker. On these issues I tend to be a kind of "chronic American." The radical separation of church and state in these areas makes me feel considerably more comfortable.

SMALL GROUP DISCUSSIONS

• • •

*This summary was prepared by **Clark Lombardi,** doctoral candidate in the Department of Religion at Columbia, who coordinated the work of the facilitators and rapporteurs before and during the conference, and systematized their written reports afterwards. For more details regarding the deliberations in small groups, and a list of facilitators and rapporteurs, please see Appendix.*

At this point the conference broke into eight small discussion groups, each facilitated by a member of the conference. Discussants were given a set of questions as a point of departure for the discussion (see Appendix). The questions dealt with the sources of human rights, the potential role of a global ethic in support of human rights, and the issues that the discussants would like to see addressed in such a document. The discussion groups were meant to be informal and discussants were encouraged to move the conversation in the direction that was of particular interest to them. Despite the great difference in perspective that participants brought to their discussion groups, the number of similar themes that emerged in the discussions was striking. Here is a brief summary of the comments stimulated by four of these issues.

How Do We Make a Global Ethic Inclusive?

Many people felt that the document *Towards a Global Ethic*, as drafted by the Parliament of the World's Religions, was not inclusive enough. In particular, the conceptual language of the draft was felt to be too Western in orientation. In addition, the use of terms such as "mankind" seem to give the document a male bias. Several discussants pointed out that the global ethic also betrayed the biases of the "progressive," ecumenical wings of the world's religions. There was uneasiness about the fact that the World Parliament of Religions (and this conference) seemed willing to ignore the exclusionary and violent world views that many people hold. This led to the question of how we could come to an agreement with people who are unwilling to enter into a dialogue about a global ethic. One conclusion was that it is important not only to recognize diversity, but to bring to every discussion a nuanced understanding of the complex differences between communities.

Enforcement of a Global Ethic

Many of the groups discussed the problematic issue of enforcing a global ethic. Most discussants felt that the notion of enforcement is antithetical to the aims of such an ethic. It was even suggested that the ethic was designed to move away from the notion of rights—a term often associated with belligerent expressions such as "fight for your rights"—as a simple and enforceable set of principles about human behavior. Rather than imposing rules from the outside, it was suggested that parents should assume the role of awakening understanding in their children. In this, organizations such as the UN could help by educating people about the value of the ethic in bettering the world, not only for all humans but for all sentient beings. There was, however, substantial doubt expressed about the possibility of educating people about the ethic, since some religious and cultural groups might not tolerate discussion of this sort. Indeed, even among discussants who expressed belief in the value of education as a tool, there was some worry that persuasion might be necessary, and the creation of a UN body to censure violations of a global ethic would be needed.

Rights versus Responsibilities

Many discussants argued that the purpose of drafting a global ethic in support of human rights is precisely to introduce "responsibility" into the guidelines for human behavior. It was suggested that "rights" insulate the individual from society, whereas "responsibilities" imply an obligation to give something back to others within society or, perhaps, to society itself. This makes "responsibility" a more effective concept than "rights" in the quest to make human societies more just, since it emphasizes the mutual interdependence of human beings. But many of the participants refused to accept the notion that "responsibility" is a broader or more effective concept than "rights." Some argued that, on the level of practice, rights and responsibilities cannot exist independently of each other.

One issue that remained unresolved is whether rights and responsibilities have different origins. Some felt that both rights and responsibilities are constructs imposed on the individual by his or her physical or social environment. Others felt that there is a notion of rights inherent in the human mind, while the notion of responsibility is a social construct that draws on this essential notion of human rights.

The Role of the Environment in a Global Ethic

Many discussants were concerned that the idea of "human rights," and even a global ethic promoting human responsibility, over-emphasize human relationships and fail to address humans' responsibilities to the environment. Many felt that any global ethic must recognize that all sentient beings have rights. This idea arose in almost every discussion. It was pointed out that the Mahayana Buddhist idea of a Buddha nature inherent in all sentient beings is a way to foster understanding and respect for the environment. Some noted that respect for the environment is present in many world views, such as the Wiccan notion that a right relationship with humans flows from a right relationship with the earth and that this relationship must be organic as the earth is organic. Others pointed out that this idea of interconnectedness and the necessity for an "organic" relationship with the environment is implicit in the concept of sustainable development. Finally, some discussants affirmed human responsibility to the environment while still focusing on "human" rights rather than human responsibilities. Thus, the discussion groups showed that there is broad support for including environmental issues in the global ethic.

Conclusion

None of the discussion groups addressed the question of specific principles to be articulated in a Global Ethic. Instead, the groups worked on important questions that will help frame the debate about a global ethic in the future:

1) Should a Global Ethic in support of human rights be a docu-

ment about human rights exclusively, or must it move on to address the notion of human responsibilities?

2) Can everyone, East or West, belligerent or pacifist, exclusivist or ecumenical, support such a document?

3) Must we enforce a Global Ethic, or is it best to try to lead through education and example?

4) Can we really talk about human rights or responsibilities without addressing humankind's stewardship of the environment upon which we all depend?

CONCLUDING REMARKS

· · ·

By Harvey Cox

Harvey G. Cox has been a member of the faculty at Harvard University since 1965. He is the Victor S. Thomas Professor of Divinity and teaches at both the Divinity School and in the Religious Studies Program of the Faculty of Arts and Sciences. Professor Cox's interests focus on the interaction of religion, politics and culture, and new religious movements. His 1965 book The Secular City, *published in eleven different languages, has sold over 900,000 copies.*

At many conferences this is the time to issue resolutions. I'm very grateful that we've decided to forego this custom. Still, having listened with gratitude throughout these hours we've been together, I have set down four resolutions of my own. These are more like New Year's resolutions than conference resolutions, but I want to mention them to you in the hope that perhaps they may spark some sense of personal resolution or intention in you.

The first is a resolution to make an even deeper commitment to the terribly important conversation between those who are involved in the protection of human rights around the world and those who are working in the field of religion. This frontier is now emerging as one of the most im-

"Those of us who spend a lot of time in the interfaith network need to spend perhaps as much time, or at least as much energy, in trying to understand those who share our own faith tradition but don't see it as something which moves them toward interfaith dialogue."

portant ones of our time. As a person speaking from a religious perspective, I think that secular people do help to keep us honest. But I also think that the secular human rights agencies have more to learn from religious traditions and religious practitioners than is evident at first blush. Some of the greatest exponents of human rights in our time—Gandhi, Martin Luther King, the Dalai Lama—are people suffused with traditional religious perspectives.

Of course, there's a shadow side, but I wonder if we might help our colleagues in the human rights organizations understand that our relationship is not necessarily one in which they must bring those of us in religious communities up to speed, so to speak. Rather, there have been insights—some of them thousands of years old—into what we now call human rights, insights that have come from the breakthroughs of the great founders and prophets and sages of the religious traditions. I think this perspective has led, and can lead, to further very fruitful conversations. I want it to continue.

My second resolution: I promised myself that I would cultivate deeper and more direct experiences of other faith traditions than my own. I underline the word experience because I am, after all, a university professor, and with the *formation professionnelle* that we all have, we tend to believe that if one reads a good book on Islam and then a good book on Buddhism, we have gotten it. I've come to be disabused of that notion after many years of teaching. I believe that all religion is based on experience. Here we are at Columbia University where John Dewey, the sage of Morningside Heights, emphasized that experience is central to human life. Experience first. After that come doctrines and institutions and ideas and after that, books about the doctrines—all fairly derivative.

We are more able now to experience the reality of the faith of those from other traditions because of what someone has called the deregionalization of religion in our world. You don't have to go to the Middle East now to worship in a mosque. There may be a mosque in your own neighborhood, no matter where you live in America. And for this I'm thankful. You don't have to go to the Far East to worship in a pagoda. But many of us, at least those of us in academic life, still rely too heavily on derivative descriptions rather than on the central experience of these faiths. I have learned over the last years that you miss something—no matter how much you read, no matter how extensively you study—unless you take that step of somehow experiencing the strangeness, but also the elation, of being with people who worship, who meditate, who pray in a different way, but with some mysterious kinship to the way you do it yourself.

Now, my third resolution is that I want to have even more direct experience of those who are the victims of oppression, of human rights violations. And once again, alas, you probably do not have to go beyond your own local community, or my local community, to share their experiences. Every community has its homeless shelter, its local legal aid association, its meals program. I've tried to spend time and be of service in those in my own community, and more and more I've come to believe those people who insist that the right to eat every day is a far more basic right than we who eat every day imagine.

The right to eat every day is extremely basic when you don't know where the meal is coming from. The right to have a place to go to escape the cold will be urgent in New York City in a few weeks, but for most of us it doesn't appear to be quite so basic. It's ironic to me that at the very time people in the former socialist countries who used to emphasize these economic and social rights are no longer doing so and are instead jumping onto the bandwagon of market economics, it is the religious communities that are now voicing these utterly basic human rights. I think it's a welcome voice.

My fourth resolution is a tough one. I've been trying to do this for years. I want to have more direct experience with what might be called the anti-dialogical wing of my own religious tradition. As a Christian, indeed as a Baptist, I know very well that such people are not hard to find. There are a lot of people, alas, in my tradition, who are not only cold to or uninterested in interfaith dialogue, but are downright against it. They have fairly well articulated reasons to be against it, to be suspicious of it. Like many of you in this room, I find it far more comfortable to converse with thoughtful Muslims and with exemplary Hindus and Buddhists than with some people in my own religious tradition who are angular and fractious and difficult and who think I'm a traitor to the faith. And yet I want to emphasize as strongly as possible that I think this is also an *enormously* important dialogue.

It has been mentioned a couple of times here that those of us who spend a lot of time in the interfaith network need to spend perhaps as much time, or at least as much energy, in trying to understand those who share our own faith tradition but don't see it as something which moves them toward interfaith dialogue. I've tried to do this. While writing the book on Pentecostalism, I found myself in some very unlikely places, including Jerry Falwell's Liberty University. I've spent time with people who are not particularly interested in interfaith dialogue, and I want to mention a couple of things that may help you if this is a resolution you would like to make.

I think we have to be very careful when we use expressions like "reaching out to these people," or "trying to bring our message" to them. When I began conversing with the anti-dialogical proponents in my own religious tradition, I found myself frequently having the very attitudes toward them that I have criticized in them—such as thinking I know what they're going to say before they say it, imposing stereotypes, thinking they're all the same, thinking they don't have any well-grounded or thought-out reason to be suspicious of what we're doing. I found I had to differentiate, disaggregate, listen. Then I realized that they are also genuinely religious human beings who, if listened to, and not just reached out to, may even have something to teach us.

Now that's a big admission for a dialogist to make. I also concede that this is a difficult task, this business of not allowing the gap between the dialogical and the non-dialogical wings of our own traditions to replace the gap that has sometimes existed between the traditions in general. Where would we be in another twenty years if we had a whole cluster of nice dialogical Muslims, Buddhists, Christians, and others over here, and all of our anti-dialogical co-religionists over there, thinking we've sold the farm—or been traitors to the Bible or the Koran or whatever else? It's important to me, and I hope it's important to you.

Last year at Harvard I organized a seminar called "Religious Values and Cultural Conflict in America." I specifically invited into that seminar graduate students at Harvard who represent the more liberal perspectives and students who are members of the Christian Coalition and the new religious right—including some Law School students. I entered upon this with fear and trembling. Would they tear each other to bits in the seminar room? Would they polemicize? Would they walk out in a rage? Break up the furniture? So I made a speech at the beginning, saying, look, if we can't talk to each other here, even about the tough issues like abortion, the so-called "gay agenda," prayer in the schools—all the things that form the agenda of the religious Right—where can anybody talk about them? And, as a bit of encouragement, I want to report that by the end of the semester they *were* able to talk to each other. There were some tough spots, and there were a couple of moments when people almost did walk out, but I have some confidence that if we understand that others have positions which require our attention, our sympathy, our genuine effort to get inside them and understand them, we can make an advance in this area as well. I intend to keep working on that.

There are my four resolutions. That's enough. I just want to end with this observation: I'm deeply grateful that we began this whole meeting with that music by Mozart. I'm grateful that after all the words have been said we are going to end with some music. Some of you already know that the great theologian Karl Barth also wrote interestingly on Mozart. He was once asked how he compared Mozart with Bach, and he said, "Well, I'm sure that when the angels gather around the throne of God to praise him, they sing Bach. But when they're just off by themselves, enjoying themselves and having a good time, I'm sure they play Mozart."

There is something about Mozart which does this for all of us, though of course Mozart, in some of his most wonderful moments, was able to speak to God as well. I think music has much to tell us. This is one of the reasons why I think worshipping in another setting, letting the music touch us, letting the imagery, the stories, the architecture, the smells as well as the books touch us, is so essential if we are going to understand and appreciate each other.

The sun is setting now over New York City, one of the great laboratories in the world for interfaith dialogue, understanding, and mutuality; and also one of the places where human rights may be greatly endangered, especially the fundamental human rights of not freezing to death or starving to death. As I stand here and look out over New York as the sun sets, I remember that I will be going home soon and the Sabbath will begin. I have a Jewish wife, so when we get home she will light the candles and spread the wine and the bread. Once again I will be thankful that I have a personal experience of a religion different than mine, but in some ways showing a deep kinship to mine, one that existed centuries and centuries before mine came along. I'm very grateful that this infinitely valuable way of getting to know another faith has come into my life. When I think that, I also think about the history that precedes it, that may go back to what Bob Thurman called the common pool of religiousness, what I call "primal spirituality," a history that links us all, links us all at some level. But it's a primal spirituality that I believe you get to through the very particular practice of your own, or my own, tradition. You arrive at that deep source through your own well.

Thank you all for being here. I was one of the people who was lucky enough at the very outset to be thinking about this conference when the Boston Center folks began talking about it. I have listened with great interest, and it has been enormously valuable for me as I'm sure it has for all of you. So I send you off with gratitude and with a wish for a Shabbat Shalom.

Closing

• • •

By Robert A.F. Thurman

Virginia Straus wanted me to say a couple of words at the end, but after the resolutions Harvey just made, I think there is hardly anything more to be said. But I kept thinking as you were talking, Harvey, about Gandhi and about something he said that always stays with me, partly for itself, but also as it reminds me of something in the *Flower Ornament Sutra*—a sort of vision of humanity. In the case of the Buddhists, it is of humanity on many planets, on multiplanets, which they had as an ancient vision.

Sometimes one feels discouraged and hopeless. Today, for example, we might think: How are we ever going to arrive at a global ethic? We think of Bosnia, Rwanda, Tibet, etc., and it just seems hopeless. But Gandhi said that in such cases he used to remind himself of the fabric of human interaction throughout the planet that goes unnoticed. Where one person extends a hand to another and hands a cup of water to another, where people sit around a table and eat dinner, where there is a common fabric of human courtesy and human consideration expressed in all cultures.

But occasionally in different places people just go totally berserk over some insane idea like, I'm a Buddhist, or I'm a Jew, or I'm a Muslim, or I'm a Serbian, or I'm a Communist, or whatever it is that the others aren't. But these are such highly exceptional cases, in a way, compared to that fabric of human kindness I was describing. Even on the day when there's a massacre in one place, billions of people are handing each other glasses of water, washing the dishes, and opening the door for each other. Maybe a hundred thousand are going crazy, but billions are doing these other things.

So what we're talking about may not be so difficult. And the human rights people may not need to feel in the typical Western way, the particularly American way, that they have to reinvent the wheel and that they have to get the UN to enforce people having table manners, for example, to hand each other pieces of bread. People are doing that everywhere, and it's just the exceptional egotists and the exceptional maniacs that have to be controlled when they have their occasional fits of ideology or whatever it is that they have. So this is just by way of encouragement. And our task is, as taken from Gandhi, to make the operators of the big machines understand the common human religion of kindness. Thank you, everyone, very much, and now, on to the music!

Nancy Roof (left) of the Values Caucus and Virginia Swain of the Coaltion for a Strong UN.

Jonathan Wilson

Sallie King (left) fields questions after her presentation.

Jonathan Wilson

Speaker Richard Falk (left) with Bawa Jain, representative of the Jain Mission.

Jonathan Wilson

Open discussion in progress.

Jonathan Wilson

An exchange of ideas and perspectives.

Jonathan Wilson

Mark Jeurgensmeyer (left) and Harvey Cox.

Jonathan Wilson

APPENDIX

• • •

Small Group Discussions

Universal Declaration of Human Rights

Towards a Global Ethic

Small Group Discussions

• • •

I. List of Facilitators and Rapporteurs

FACILITATORS

Professor John Cort
Department of Religion
Columbia University

Fr. Luis M. Dolan
Temple of Understanding

Andrew Gebert
Soka Gakkai International

P.N. (Bawa) Jain
International Mahavir Jain Mission

Ron Kassimir
Assistant Director
Institute for African Studies
Columbia University

Professor Dan Madigan
Department of Religion
Columbia University

Professor Gurinder Singh Mann
Department of Religion
Columbia University

Professor Mary McGee
Department of Religion
Vassar College

RAPPORTEURS

Hicham Aidi
Department of Political Science
Columbia University

Anna Bigelow
Department of Religion
Columbia University

David Gray
Department of Religion
Columbia University

Jim Hartzell
Department of Religion
Columbia University

Robert Morrison
Department of Middle East and
    Asian Languages and Cultures
Columbia University

Amir Parsa
Department of English and
Comparative Literature

Jenny Seymore
Department of Middle East and
    Asian Languages and Cultures
Columbia University

Tom Yarnall
Department of Religion
Columbia University

II. Questions offered as possible starting points for the small group discussions (The eight groups were given an hour and a half to discuss one of these questions or one of their own choice. The conference then reconvened in a plenary session moderated by Professor Mark Juergensmeyer to hear the results of the discussion as presented by the rapporteurs and facilitators.):

A. Definition of the Global Ethic

   Thought experiment: Imagine that a statement of a global ethic has been articulated to support the Universal Declaration of Human Rights. Does the global ethic you envision resemble the initial declaration adopted by the Council for a Parliament of the World's Religions?

B. The Source of Human Rights

   1) What rights do you feel are so basic that they would be accepted by peoples of all religious and ideological backgrounds? Where are these values articulated in society: in religious texts? in constitutions or laws? in cultural traditions?
   2) Select one right that the group agrees upon as a "human right," such as the right not to be enslaved. How did we come to appreciate this right? through common sense? through religious teaching? through the laws of our nation?
   3) *Towards a Global Ethic* is an interfaith declaration. Are its contents in accord with secular values? If not, would the declaration require substantive revision to encompass them?

C. The Purpose of a Statement of Global Ethic

   1) Consider a specific human rights struggle such as the civil rights movement in the US from the 1950s to the present. How might such a movement have been affected by the presence of a statement of global ethic that was embraced by the world's religions?
   2) Debate the following: A global ethic is required to buttress the United Nations 1948 Universal Declaration of Human Rights.

III. Reports at the plenary

Juergensmeyer: This is our chance to find out what the groups have discussed during the past hour or so. From what I've heard so far, these have been lively, interesting discussions, sparked by some stimulating questions on the definition of a global ethic, the sources of human rights, and the purpose of the statement on a global ethic. The conversation seems to have ranged over all sorts of things from that fragile starting point, and that's what we want to find out about now.

Hicham Aidi: My group, which was facilitated by Dr. Mary McGee, used question B.1 as a means of focusing on the problem of common values. One member of the group argued that the problem we are facing is not a lack of common values, but the absence of a higher authority to enforce them. As she put it, there is no Santa Claus who can ensure that conflicts are resolved in a peaceful manner or who can enforce this issue of human rights. The counter proposition was that the problem is not the lack of a higher authority, but the difficulty in getting people to unite in their respect for the mystery and the sanctity of life. After all, there is no lack of ethical models—every religion has its ethics. What is it, then, about our societies which precludes us from recognizing the common values we already have?

This question led to a discussion about sensitivity to language. During this conference there have been frequent references to "mankind's" human rights, but this term seems a bit too gender-specific; many of the terms used in these discussions are biased towards men. There is also a more general area in which language could create other difficulties. For example, if you use the expression, "fight for your rights," that is an indirect encouragement to violence, or at least it could be interpreted as such. So, we would recommend a cautious use of language. We also recognized that words don't necessarily lead to nice behavior—there is a yawning gap between creed and deed.

One of our speakers astutely pointed out that there is an important difference between "human rights" and a "global ethic." The concept of human rights is narrower than that of a global ethic. The notion of a "global ethic" is more comprehensive than "human rights" because the latter does not speak about responsibilities, yet responsibilities are an implicit part of living with other people. The concept of human rights may be too individualized. As one of our speakers asked, if I were alone in a jungle, would I have any rights? Or do rights arise when I'm living in a society with other people? Our conclusion was that the notion of rights needs a broader foundation, one that deals with the individual as a member of a society rather than alone. A global ethic can capture this.

Another concern was that many people at this conference—people who signed this declaration of a global ethic—represent only the liberal end of their cultural traditions. There are few representatives of the more conservative traditions. How do we reach out to these people? How do we establish a dialogue with them? In order to accomplish this, the discussion must be brought down to the local level, and linked to tangible programs of action. Such programs are essential to bringing the dialogue on ethics into relation with the reality of people's lives.

Perhaps we need workshops that could be used to criticize and debate particular points of this document. Then we could have updated versions of the documents and minutes of these discussions mailed out to religious bodies everywhere and to various international organizations— even, as one person suggested, to the World Bank and the IMF. We also need to find a way to teach our children ethics without the religious trappings. These might be embodied in stories or myths that cut across religious and cultural traditions and that allow each culture to develop notions such as that of "nonviolence" in its own way. The motto, "think globally, act locally," is an important point of reference in all these activities.

Anna Bigelow: Professor Cort was our facilitator. Our main focus was on the question of rights in relation to responsibilities. What is their nature, and what is their relationship? Are they related, are they inalienable, are they natural or cultural? The question of nature and nurture was a major theme in our discussion.

Professor Wayman asserted that rights derive from birth and that one can claim them by virtue of being alive. Others suggested that rights and responsibilities are social contracts, while a third possibility is that rights are essentially political in origin, whereas responsibilities are social. The Buddhist imperative of responsibility and responsiveness was addressed at some length, and it was then suggested that responsibility is what puts a theory of rights into action.

We then asked what our responsibilities in a global society are, and moved from there to a discussion of inalienable basic rights. This again led to the question of whether human rights are culturally relative and the danger in focusing on attitudes held in common without a complex and nuanced understanding of real and important differences. Still, we felt that some of the notions certain religions espouse might be very powerful and productive terms to introduce into the debate, such as the Buddha nature and the interconnectedness of nature and society that are also present in many indigenous religions. Our discussion ended with the problem of how to bridge the gap between those willing to accommodate discussion and those who are intolerant of such discussion.

David Gray: Our group, led by Bawa Jain, began with the question of the definition of a global ethic. We came to the conclusion that we weren't going to make any resolutions on this question. Instead we decided to investigate the basis for such an ethic. What does it involve? Some people felt that such an ethic is somehow preexistent, but there was a larger group that felt this view is somehow part of the problem that we're facing. The tendency for humans to reify things, to see an ethic or a religious tradition as static and unchanging precludes further discussion or understanding. Rather than espousing this sort of view, in any discussion of a human ethic we need to start from the idea that it is not part of a set of fixed rules, but something that is evolving, something that we are creating through the process of human dialogue. It isn't going to come out of a collision of monolithic religions or institutions that are antithetical to each other. It can only come into being if people with different ideas and different views meet with the idea of exploring and coming to a new understanding together.

Secondly, concerning the source of a global ethic, even though we resolved not to make a resolution, there seemed to be some agreement that a global ethic brings with it the notion of compassion, of there being some sort of intrinsic value in all life, human life in particular. We have to find some way to bring about the evolution of an ethic that supports, engenders, and even, perhaps, enforces this. Concerning how to do this, it seemed that the family is essential. Some people felt that women—mothers in particular—are a central source of ethical instruction for children, but others felt that we shouldn't shift the whole burden of this onto women. Men, too, can be positive, empowering parents. The education of both children and adults should include learning about different religious traditions so as to engender tolerance and understanding.

Finally, we felt that the UN must play a crucial role in the development of a global ethic. It was felt that, in our increasingly globalized world, the UN must be empowered and funded to help determine these issues. It could also help define a truly international form of government based on this ethic.

Jim Hartzell: In Father Dolan's group, we left aside the question of what a global ethic is, since we more or less assumed that it already exists. Instead, we went on to focus more on the issue of promoting and implementing this global ethic. How would you actually apply it in the real world? There was real disagreement on this point. On one side, we had advocates of some sort of global enforcement of the ethic, just as you have national enforcement of national laws, or religious enforcement of religious doctrines. This might mean the deployment of a global military force to intervene and prevent violations. There was very strong consensus in the opposite direction, though. Fear of authoritarian intervention was expressed, and the desire to create a viable and practical approach to a global ethic that begins with the individual were the grounds for this consensus. It was specifically suggested that the individual should begin in his or her community, whether academic, religious, social, or professional, in an attempt to incorporate some of the values found in the global ethic in the group's practice.

For example, if you are a minister, you could try to address some of the more extreme elements in your Christian tradition, those less tolerant of other groups; or if you're a Muslim imam, you might want to address some of the more radical elements in Islam. The point is to really try to work outward from within rather than trying to start with a large global idea and enforcing it on everybody.

Regarding the media and a global ethic, there was a general consensus that, at the moment, the media would rather focus on things like the O.J. Simpson trial. However, some of these ideas might be communicated through media forums such as talk shows, educational programming, special events, as well as through the arts. For example, given the negative ideas that have recently been propagated about Islam, the community could stage public events that would convey the larger ethical commitment to mercy and compassion that is central to the religion.

Robert Morrison: In Professor Dan Madigan's group, we used question B.2 as a jumping-off point for a discussion of how we come to appreciate a right. What inside us makes us feel that every person has the right not to be enslaved? Someone immediately said, Christianity says this, Islam says this. But given the experience of African-Americans in this country and the slavery in Islamic lands, there's a gap between reality and ideals.

From this we moved to a more theoretical level. How exactly do we appreciate or understand this? Some people seemed to feel that we get it from individual experience—that is, a sense that certain things are our rights—and not through something programmatic. Other members of our group disagreed, saying that it does come from something programmatic. In fact, in the West, in the US, it comes from our sense of law, specifically our Constitution. The point was raised that Americans see the law not just as secular law, but as something almost supernatural. That is why we feel free to enter other countries, like Haiti, in order to enforce democracy. Americans seem to ground the concept of fundamental rights in the references to the Creator in the Declaration of Independence.

At this point we took up the question of the relation of "rights" to law. Modern Western societies and more traditional religious communities might find some common ground in a comparative understanding of law and its sources in religion. This led to a discussion of minimalist and maximalist options. Some people saw in the minimalist ethic a possibility for agreement, whereas a maximalist ethic allows no room for discussion. A minimalist ethic, once agreed upon, would open the way to a dialogue on the knottier issues found in maximalist demands. The suggestion was made again that law might provide the initial vocabulary for such a dialogue.

Amir Parsa: I'll just briefly sketch out some of the questions that came up in Singh Mann's group. First, we all agreed from the beginning that we are basically what you could call liberals—at least we are willing to sit down and speak to each other, and we are interested in community life and in bettering it. That was already a starting point.

We went on to discuss how, instead of having a lot of legislation at the community or national level, we could model our behavior in terms of the way we believe people should behave, or how we would want them to behave. In other words, there can't be a philosophy of ethics without first illustrating that ethic yourself. We must model ethical behavior. A second point was that, instead of the grand proposals and declarations that come out of meetings at grand hotels, we should have communities coming together to create dialogues in which all could participate.

This led us to think about participatory models rather than about reading or disseminating documents. We asked what those models might look like and how we could produce them. Important here was the problem of the "expert," or of authority, whether religious or legislative. To circumvent authoritarian imposition of rules, the dissemination of ethical norms has to take place elsewhere, through other organs. In this context, it is important to create models in which minority groups of whatever kind and within whatever structure—groups that have no power or any authority representing them—could have a voice.

We also raised a few other pragmatic issues. One was the internalization of values. Where do we begin our discussion of values in the real world? A few people thought that we should just talk in small communities, in small groups. Another pragmatic option was to take surveys in various countries to see whether there are really values that everybody agrees about. The final issue we touched on, specifically in relation to women, is how to deal with the problem of not even having the possibility of dialogue. There are nations and structures in which even the thought of wanting to dissent or to speak is not allowed, is blasphemous. What do you do in a case when you're not even allowed to think that you may or may not have a right? What kind of action do you take: violent, nonviolent, tolerant, intolerant? How do you dissent when you can't even formulate the idea?

Jenny Seymore: In Andrew Gebert's group we began with question B.1. A doctor suggested that the right to health care and disease prevention was among the most basic of human rights. The disagreement that arose when this was applied to specific cultures and religions led to a discussion of the issue of religious education. Group members felt that their ignorance of other religious traditions, beliefs, and ethics was due to the lack of religious education in American schools. There are, however, dangers in allowing religious education, since false ideas can be disseminated as fact in such a context. And the fear people have of "the other," of the blurring of boundaries, must be recognized and corrected.

This led us directly to the question of the pragmatics of dealing with others who are very different from ourselves and who work within different discourses. In looking for ways of dealing with this fear, someone said that education about the religions of the world is really what can help us to cross these barriers and speak to one another. That brought us back to Article 18 of the Universal Declaration of Human Rights. Do all people in the world have the right to examine their own religion and to change their religion if they feel that's appropriate?

Some discussion followed on the uses and abuses of a global ethic, should one come into being. Some expressed fear that it would be used in an overly normative fashion, to bring "others" in line with a liberal, Western set of values. Others felt the global ethic has meaning on a private basis, as a jumping-off point for inquiry: a learning tool, a blueprint to address the issues at hand, a description of an ideal set of ethics upon which to focus. Despite the difficulties of formulating a draft upon which all religious leaders can agree, the group felt the effort was worthwhile, and that the difficulties should be worked through in order to get to the next stage of discussion on global human rights.

Tom Yarnall: Ron Kassimir's group began by acknowledging the importance of dialogue. The phrase "tolerating diversity" was mentioned this morning, and someone suggested that this is not really a choice we have. We do not have a choice about whether we should value the tolerance of diversity in the interconnected political environment we have today. Since this is no longer a choice, what we're doing here today is very important.

We then moved on to what it means to have the right to live, whether that could be considered a basic right that everyone can agree on. We devoted a lot of our discussion to examining the language of this question. We considered the possibility of changing "the right to live" to include the right to belong, whether it be to a single-family group or the human race as a whole. The right to live is perhaps necessary, but not sufficient. From an anthropological point of view, the right to survive is something different from just the right to live, because being alive doesn't mean that your circumstances are sufficient. We then included as part of this discussion the problem of what it means to have a right in the first place. Is it appropriate to talk of these issues in terms of rights, or are they really needs? What's the difference between a right and a need? We then moved on to the issue of the right to be free and a discussion of physical freedom. Freedom not to be enslaved is based in freedoms of a more abstract sort—freedom of speech, freedom to dissent, freedom to feel it's safe to express dissent without being punished.

The other topic that we felt very important is the issue of inclusion. There was some discomfort expressed about the fact that not everybody has felt completely included in the dialogue. Some people did not sign the document because they felt it was too Western in orientation. Some others did not sign it because, for example, the initial declaration did not define the context: Who is the "we"? Who is declaring all this? It will be important to develop language that is more inclusive of people from the West and the East, so that the fruits of this dialogue can be shared more broadly.

Juergensmeyer: I am impressed by the number of themes that were brought up earlier that continued on into these discussions. I was also impressed with the number of new things that came up. For example, in a number of these reports there were references to what might be called the dark side of global ethics. If there's going to be a global ethics, whose global ethics? And is there an implicit homogenization of world culture here? Is there a kind of "McDonaldization" of ethics lurking in the background, one in which it is assumed the world would be better if everybody were more like "us," whoever "us" is? I also heard a plea for the tolerance of diversity of values, but within some common understanding of the family of humanity.

Universal Declaration of Human Rights*

• • •

Introduction

On 10 December 1948, the General Assembly of the United Nations adopted and proclaimed the Universal Declaration of Human Rights, the full text of which appears in the following pages. Following this historic act, the Assembly called upon all Member countries to publicize the text of the Declaration and "to cause it to be disseminated, displayed, read and expounded principally in schools and other educational institutions, without distinction based on the political status of countries or territories."

—Boutros Boutros-Ghali
Secretary-General

All human beings are born with equal and inalienable rights and fundamental freedoms.

The United Nations is committed to upholding, promoting and protecting the human rights of every individual. This commitment stems the United Nations Charter, which reaffirms the faith of the peoples of the world in fundamental human rights and in the dignity and worth of the human person.

In the Universal Declaration of Human Rights, the United Nations has stated in clear and simple terms the rights which belong equally to every person.

These rights belong to you.

They are your rights.

Familiarize yourself with them. Help to promote and defend them for yourself as well as for your fellow human beings.

Preamble

Whereas recognition of the inherent dignity and of the equal and inalienable rights of all members of the human family is the foundation of freedom, justice and peace in the world,

---

* UN Publications Sales #DPI/876.

Whereas disregard and contempt for human rights have resulted in barbarous acts which have outraged the conscience of mankind, and the advent of a world in which human beings shall enjoy freedom of speech and belief and freedom from fear and want has been proclaimed as the highest aspiration of the common people,

Whereas it is essential, if man is not to be compelled to have recourse, as a last resort, to rebellion against tyranny and oppression, that human rights should be protected by the rule of law,

Whereas it is essential to promote the development of friendly relations between nations,

Whereas the peoples of the United Nations have in the Charter reaffirmed their faith in fundamental human rights, in the dignity and worth of the human person and in the equal rights of men and women and have determined to promote social progress and better standards of life in larger freedom,

Whereas Member States have pledged themselves to achieve, in cooperation with the United Nations, the promotion of universal respect for and observance of human rights and fundamental freedoms,

Whereas a common understanding of these rights and freedoms is of the greatest importance for the full realization of this pledge,

Now, Therefore,
The General Assembly
proclaims
This Universal Declaration
of Human Rights

as a common standard of achievement for all peoples and all nations, to the end that every individual and every organ of society, keeping this Declaration constantly in mind, shall strive by teaching and education to promote respect for these rights and freedoms and by progressive measures, national and international, to secure their universal and effective recognition and observance, both among the peoples of Member States themselves and among the peoples of territories under their jurisdiction.

Article I

All human beings are born free and equal in dignity and rights. They are endowed with reason and conscience and should act towards one another in a spirit of brotherhood.

Article 2

Everyone is entitled to all the rights and freedoms set forth in this Declaration, without distinction of any kind, such as race, colour, sex, language, religion, political or other opinion, national or social origin, property, birth or other status.

Furthermore, no distinction shall be made on the basis of the political, jurisdictional or international status of the country or territory to which a person belongs, whether it be independent, trust, non-selfgoverning or under any other limitation of sovereignty.

Article 3

Everyone has the right to life, liberty and security of person.

Article 4

No one shall be held in slavery or servitude; slavery and the slave trade shall be prohibited in all their forms.

Article 5

No one shall be subjected to torture or to cruel, inhuman or degrading treatment or punishment.

Article 6

Everyone has the right to recognition everywhere as a person before the law.

Article 7

All are equal before the law and are entitled without any discrimination to equal protection of the law. All are entitled to equal protection against any discrimination in violation of this Declaration and against any incitement to such discrimination.

Article 8

Everyone has the right to an effective remedy by the competent national tribunals for acts violating the fundamental rights granted him by the constitution or by law.

Article 9

No one shall be subjected to arbitrary arrest, detention or exile.

Article 10

Everyone is entitled in full equality to a fair and public hearing by an

independent and impartial tribunal, in the determination of his rights and
obligations and of any criminal charge against him.

Article 11

(1) Everyone charged with a penal offence has the right to be pre-
sumed innocent until proved guilty according to law in a public trial at
which he has had all the guarantees necessary for his defence.

(2) No one shall be held guilty of any penal offence on account of any
act or omission which did not constitute a penal offence, under national or
international law, at the time when it was committed. Nor shall a heavier
penalty be imposed than the one that was applicable at the time the penal
offence was committed.

Article 12

No one shall be subjected to arbitrary interference with his privacy,
family, home or correspondence, nor to attacks upon his honour and repu-
tation. Everyone has the right to the protection of the law against such
interference or attacks.

Article 13

(1) Everyone has the right to freedom of movement and residence
within the borders of each State.

(2) Everyone has the right to leave any country, including his own,
and to return to his country.

Article 14

(1) Everyone has the right to seek and to enjoy in other countries asy-
lum from persecution.

(2) This right may not be invoked in the case of prosecutions genuinely arising from non-political crimes or from acts contrary to the purposes and principles of the United Nations.

Article 15

(1) Everyone has the right to a nationality.

(2) No one shall be arbitrarily deprived of his nationality nor denied
the right to change his nationality.

Article 16

(1) Men and women of full age, without any limitation due to race,

nationality or religion, have the right to marry and to found a family. They are entitled to equal rights as to marriage, during marriage and at its dissolution.

(2) Marriage shall be entered into only with the free and full consent of the intending spouses.

(3) The family is the natural and fundamental group unit of society and is entitled to protection by society and the State.

Article 17

(1) Everyone has the right to own property alone as well as in association with others.

(2) No one shall be arbitrarily deprived of his property.

Article 18

Everyone has the right to freedom of thought, conscience and religion; this right includes freedom to change his religion or belief, and freedom, either alone or in community with others and in public or private, to manifest his religion or belief in teaching, practice, worship and observance.

Article 19

Everyone has the right to freedom of opinion and expression; this right includes freedom to hold opinions without interference and to seek, receive and impart information and ideas through any media and regardless of frontiers.

Article 20

(1) Everyone has the right to freedom of peaceful assembly and association.

(2) No one may be compelled to belong to an association.

Article 21

(1) Everyone has the right to take part in the government of his country, directly or through freely chosen representatives.

(2) Everyone has the right of equal access to public service in his country.

(3) The will of the people shall be the basis of the authority of government; this will shall be expressed in periodic and genuine elections which shall be by universal and equal suffrage and shall be held by secret vote or by equivalent free voting procedures.

Article 22

Everyone, as a member of society, has the right to social security and is entitled to realization, through national effort and international co-operation and in accordance with the organization and resources of each State, of the economic, social and cultural rights indispensable for his dignity and the free development of his personality.

Article 23

(1) Everyone has the right to work, to free choice of employment, to just and favourable conditions of work and to protection against unemployment.

(2) Everyone, without any discrimination, has the right to equal pay for equal work.

(3) Everyone who works has the right to just and favourable remuneration ensuring for himself and his family an existence worthy of human dignity, and supplemented, if necessary, by other means of social protection.

(4) Everyone has the right to form and to join trade unions for the protection of his interests.

Article 24

Everyone has the right to rest and leisure, including reasonable limitation of working hours and periodic holidays with pay.

Article 25

(1) Everyone has the right to a standard of living adequate for the health and well-being of himself and of his family, including food, clothing, housing and medical care and necessary social services, and the right to security in the event of unemployment, sickness, disability, widowhood, old age or other lack of livelihood in circumstances beyond his control.

(2) Motherhood and childhood are entitled to special care and assistance. All children, whether born in or out of wedlock, shall enjoy the same social protection.

Article 26

(1) Everyone has the right to education. Education shall be free, at least in the elementary and fundamental stages. Elementary education shall be compulsory. Technical and professional education shall be made generally available and higher education shall be equally accessible to all on the basis of merit.

(2) Education shall be directed to the full development of the human personality and to the strengthening of respect for human rights and fundamental freedoms. It shall promote understanding, tolerance and friendship among all nations, racial or religious groups, and shall further the activities of the United Nations for the maintenance of peace.

(3) Parents have a prior right to choose the kind of education that shall be given to their children.

Article 27

(1) Everyone has the right freely to participate in the cultural life of the community, to enjoy the arts and to share in scientific advancement and its benefits.

(2) Everyone has the right to the protection of the moral and material interests resulting from any scientific, literary or artistic production of which he is the author.

Article 28

Everyone is entitled to a social and international order in which the rights and freedoms set forth in this Declaration can be fully realized.

Article 29

(1) Everyone has duties to the community in which alone the free and full development of his personality is possible.

(2) In the exercise of his rights and freedoms, everyone shall be subject only to such limitations as are determined by law solely for the purpose of securing due recognition and respect for the rights and freedoms of others and of meeting the just requirements of morality, public order and the general welfare in a democratic society.

(3) These rights and freedoms may in no case be exercised contrary to the purposes and principles of the United Nations.

Article 30

Nothing in this Declaration may be interpreted as implying for any State, group or person any right to engage in any activity or to perform any act aimed at the destruction of any of the rights and freedoms set forth herein.

Towards a Global Ethic
(An Initial Declaration)

1993 Parliament of the World's Religions
Chicago, Illinois, USA

• • •

This interfaith declaration is the result of a two-year consultation among scholars and theologians representing the world's communities of faith.

On September 2-4, 1993, the document was discussed by an assembly of religious and spiritual leaders meeting as part of the 1993 Parliament of the World's Religions in Chicago. Respected leaders from all the world's major faiths signed the declaration as individuals, agreeing that it represents an initial effort: a point of beginning for a world sorely in need of ethical consensus.

The Council for a Parliament of the World's Religions and the persons who have endorsed this text offer it to the world as an initial statement of those rules for living on which the world's religions agree.

For more information, please write to the Council for a Parliament of the World's Religions, P.O. Box 1630, Chicago, IL 60690.

The Declaration of a Global Ethic

The world is in agony. The agony is so pervasive and urgent that we are compelled to name its manifestations so that the depth of this pain may be made clear.

Peace eludes us ... the planet is being destroyed ... neighbors live in fear ... women and men are estranged from each other ... children die!
This is abhorrent!
We condemn the abuses of Earth's ecosystems.
We condemn the poverty that stifles life's potential; the hunger that

weakens the human body; the economic disparities that threaten so many families with ruin.

We condemn the social disarray of the nations; the disregard for justice which pushes citizens to the margin; the anarchy overtaking our communities; and the insane death of children from violence. In particular we condemn aggression and hatred in the name of religion.

But this agony need not be.

It need not be because the basis for an ethic already exists. This ethic offers the possibility of a better individual and global order, and leads individuals away from despair and societies away from chaos.

We are women and men who have embraced the precepts and practices of the world's religions.

We affirm that a common set of core values is found in the teachings of the religions, and that these form the basis of a global ethic.

We affirm that this truth is already known, but yet to be lived in heart and action.

We affirm that there is an irrevocable, unconditional norm for all areas of life, for families and communities, for races, nations, and religions. There already exist ancient guidelines for human behavior which are found in the teachings of the religions of the world and which are the condition for a sustainable world order.

We Declare:

We are interdependent. Each of us depends on the well-being of the whole, and so we have respect for the community of living beings, for people, animals, and plants, and for the preservation of Earth, the air, water and soil.

We take individual responsibility for all we do. All our decisions, actions, and failures to act have consequences.

We must treat others as we wish others to treat us. We make a commitment to respect life and dignity, individuality and diversity, so that every person is treated humanely, without exception. We must have patience and acceptance. We must be able to forgive, learning from the past but never allowing ourselves to be enslaved by memories of hate. Opening our hearts to one another, we must sink our narrow differences for the cause of the world community, practicing a culture of solidarity and relatedness.

We consider humankind our family. We must strive to be kind and generous. We must not live for ourselves alone, but should also serve others, never forgetting the children, the aged, the poor, the suffering, the disabled, the refugees, and the lonely. No person should ever be considered or treated as a second-class citizen, or be exploited in any way whatsoever. There should be equal partnership between men and women. We must not commit any kind of sexual immorality. We must put behind us all forms of domination or abuse.

We commit ourselves to a culture of nonviolence, respect, justice, and peace. We shall not oppress, injure, torture, or kill other human beings, forsaking violence as a means of settling differences.

We must strive for a just social and economic order, in which everyone has an equal chance to reach full potential as a human being. We must speak and act truthfully and with compassion, dealing fairly with all, and avoiding prejudice and hatred. We must not steal. We must move beyond the dominance of greed for power, prestige, money, and consumption to make a just and peaceful world.

Earth cannot be changed for the better unless the consciousness of individuals is changed first. We pledge to increase our awareness by disciplining our minds, by meditation, by prayer, or by positive thinking. Without risk and a readiness to sacrifice there can be no fundamental change in our situation. Therefore we commit ourselves to this global ethic, to understanding one another, and to socially beneficial, peace-fostering, and nature-friendly ways of life.

We invite all people, whether religious or not, to do the same.

The Principles of a Global Ethic

Our world is experiencing a fundamental crisis: a crisis in global economy, global ecology, and global politics. The lack of a grand vision, the tangle of unresolved problems, political paralysis, mediocre political leadership with little insight or foresight, and in general too little sense for the commonweal are seen everywhere: too many old answers to new challenges.

Hundreds of millions of human beings on our planet increasingly suffer from unemployment, poverty, hunger, and the destruction of their families. Hope for a lasting peace among nations slips away from us. There are tensions between the sexes and generations. Children die, kill, and are killed. More and more countries are shaken by corruption in politics and business. It is increasingly difficult to live together peacefully in our cities because of social, racial, and ethnic conflicts, the abuse of drugs, organized crime, and even anarchy. Even neighbors often live in fear of one another. Our planet continues to be ruthlessly plundered. A collapse of the ecosystem threatens us.

Time and again we see leaders and members of religions incite aggression, fanaticism, hate, and xenophobia–even inspire and legitimize violent and bloody conflicts. Religion often is misused for purely power-political goals, including war. We are filled with disgust.

We condemn these blights and declare that they need not be. An ethic already exists within the religious teachings of the world which can counter the global distress. Of course, this ethic provides no direct solution for all the immense problems of the world, but it does supply the moral foundation for a better individual and global order: a vision which can lead women and men away from despair and society away from chaos.

We are persons who have committed ourselves to the precepts and practices of the world's religions. We confirm that there is already a consensus among the religions which can be the basis for a global ethic–a minimal *fundamental consensus* concerning binding *values*, irrevocable *standards*, and *fundamental moral attitudes.*

I.   No new global order without a new global ethic!

We women and men of various religions and regions of Earth therefore address all people, religious and nonreligious. We wish to express the following convictions which we hold in common:
   • We all have a responsibility for a better global order.
   • Our involvement for the sake of human rights, freedom, justice, peace, and the preservation of Earth is absolutely necessary.
   • Our different religious and cultural traditions must not prevent our common involvement in opposing all forms of inhumanity and working for greater humaneness.
   • The principles expressed in this Global Ethic can be affirmed by all persons with ethical convictions, whether religiously grounded or not.
   • As religious and spiritual persons we base our lives on an Ultimate Reality, and draw spiritual power and hope therefrom, in trust, in prayer or meditation, in word or silence. We have a special responsibility for the welfare of all humanity and care for the planet Earth. We do not consider ourselves better than other women and men, but we trust that the ancient wisdom of our religions can point the way for the future.

After two world wars and the end of the cold war, the collapse of fascism and nazism, the shaking to the foundations of communism and colonialism, humanity has entered a new phase of its history. Today we possess sufficient economic, cultural, and spiritual resources to introduce a better global order. But old and new ethnic, national, social, economic, and religious tensions threaten the peaceful building of a better world. We have experienced greater technological progress than ever before, yet we see that worldwide poverty, hunger, death of children, unemployment, misery, and the destruction of nature have not diminished but rather have increased. Many peoples are threatened with economic ruin, social disarray, political marginalization, ecological catastrophe, and national collapse.

In such a dramatic global situation, humanity needs a vision of peoples living peacefully together, of ethnic and ethical groupings and of religions

126

sharing responsibility for the care of Earth. A vision rests on hopes, goals, ideals, standards. But all over the world these have slipped from our hands. Yet we are convinced that, despite their frequent abuses and failures, it is the communities of faith who bear a responsibility to demonstrate that such hopes, ideals, and standards can be guarded, grounded, and lived. This is especially true in the modern state. Guarantees of freedom of conscience and religion are necessary, but they do not substitute for binding values, convictions, and norms which are valid for all humans regardless of their social origin, sex, skin color, language, or religion.

We are convinced of the fundamental unity of the human family on Earth. We recall the 1948 Universal Declaration of Human Rights of the United Nations. What it formally proclaimed on the level of rights we wish to confirm and deepen here from the perspective of an ethic: the full realization of the intrinsic dignity of the human person, the inalienable freedom and equality in principle of all humans, and the necessary solidarity and interdependence of all humans with each other.

On the basis of personal experiences and the burdensome history of our planet, we have learned:

• that a better global order cannot be created or enforced by laws, prescriptions, and conventions alone;

• that the realization of peace, justice, and the protection of Earth depends on the insight and readiness of men and women to act justly;

• that action in favor of rights and freedoms presumes a consciousness of responsibility and duty, and that therefore both the minds and hearts of women and men must be addressed;

• that rights without morality cannot long endure, and that *there will be no better global order without a global ethic.*

By a global ethic we do not mean a global ideology or a single unified religion beyond all existing religions, and certainly not the domination of one religion over all others. By a global ethic we mean a fundamental consensus on binding values, irrevocable standards, and personal attitudes. Without such a fundamental consensus on an ethic, sooner or later every community will be threatened by chaos or dictatorship, and individuals will despair.

II. A fundamental demand: Every human being must be treated humanely.

We all are fallible, imperfect men and women with limitations and defects. We know the reality of evil. Precisely because of this, we feel compelled for the sake of global welfare to express what the fundamental elements of a global ethic should be–for individuals as well as for communities and organizations, for states as well as for the religions themselves. We trust that our often millennia-old religious and ethical traditions provide"an ethic which is convincing and practicable for all women and men of good will, religious and nonreligious.

At the same time we know that our various religious and ethical traditions often offer very different bases for what is helpful and what is unhelpful for men and women, what is right and what is wrong, what is good and what is evil. We do not wish to gloss over or ignore the serious differences among the individual religions. However, they should not hinder us from proclaiming publicly those things which we already hold in common and which we jointly affirm, each on the basis of our own religious or ethical grounds.

We know that religions cannot solve the environmental, economic, political, and social problems of Earth. However, they can provide what obviously cannot be attained by economic plans, political programs, or legal regulations alone: a change in the inner orientation, the whole mentality, the "hearts" of people, and a conversion from a false path to a new orientation for life. Humankind urgently needs social and ecological reforms, but it needs spiritual renewal just as urgently. As religious or spiritual persons we commit ourselves to this task. The spiritual powers of the religions can offer a fundamental sense of trust, a ground of meaning, ultimate standards, and a spiritual home. Of course, religions are credible only when they eliminate those conflicts which spring from the religions themselves, dismantling mutual arrogance, mistrust, prejudice, and even hostile images, and thus demonstrate respect for the traditions, holy places, feasts, and rituals of people who believe differently.

Now as before, women and men are treated inhumanely all over the world. They are robbed of their opportunities and their freedom; their human rights are trampled underfoot; their dignity is disregarded. But might does not make right! In the face of all inhumanity our religious and ethical convictions demand that *every human being must be treated humanely!*

This means that every human being without distinction of age, sex, race, skin color, physical or mental ability, language, religion, political view, or national or social origin possesses an inalienable and untouchable dignity, and everyone, the individual as well as the state, is therefore obliged to honor this dignity and protect it. Humans must always be the subjects of rights, must be ends, never mere means, never objects of commercialization and industrialization in economics, politics and media, in research institutes, and industrial corporations. No one stands "above good and evil"–no human being, no social class, no influential interest group, no cartel, no police apparatus, no army, and no state. On the contrary, possessed of reason and conscience, every human is obliged to behave in a genuinely human fashion, to do good and avoid evil!

It is the intention of this Global Ethic to clarify what this means. In it we wish to recall irrevocable, unconditional ethical norms. These should not be bonds and chains, but helps and supports for people to find and realize once again their lives' direction, values, orientations, and meaning.

There is a principle which is found and has persisted in many religious and ethical traditions of humankind for thousands of years: *What you do not wish done to yourself, do not do to others.* Or in positive terms: *What you wish done to yourself, do to others!* This should be the irrevocable, unconditional norm for all areas of life, for families and communities, for races, nations, and religions.

Every form of egoism should be rejected: All selfishness, whether individual or collective, whether in the form of class thinking, racism, nationalism, or sexism. We condemn these because they prevent humans from being authentically human. Self-determination and self-realization are thoroughly legitimate so long as they are not separated from human self-responsibility and global responsibility, that is, from responsibility for fellow humans and for the planet Earth.

This principle implies very concrete standards to which we humans should hold firm. From it arise four broad, ancient guidelines for human behavior which are found in most of the religions of the world.

III. Irrevocable directives.

1. Commitment to a Culture of Nonviolence and Respect for Life.

Numberless women and men of all regions and religions strive to lead lives not determined by egoism but by commitment to their fellow humans and to the world around them. Nevertheless, all over the world we find endless hatred, envy, jealousy, and violence, not only between individuals but also between social and ethnic groups, between classes, races, nations, and religions. The use of violence, drug trafficking and organized crime, often equipped with new technical possibilities, has reached global proportions. Many places still are ruled by terror "from above;" dictators oppress their own people, and institutional violence is widespread. Even in some countries where laws exist to protect individual freedoms, prisoners are tortured, men and women are mutilated, hostages are killed.

a) In the great ancient religious and ethical traditions of humankind we find the directive: *You shall not kill!* Or in positive terms: *Have respect for life!* Let us reflect anew on the consequences of this ancient directive: All people have a right to life, safety, and the free development of personality insofar as they do not injure the rights of others. No one has the right physically or psychically to torture, injure, much less kill, any other human being. And no people, no state, no race, no religion has the right to hate, to discriminate against, to "cleanse," to exile, much less to liquidate a "foreign" minority which is different in behavior or holds different beliefs.

b)   Of course, wherever there are humans there will be conflicts. Such conflicts, however, should be resolved without violence within a framework of justice. This is true for states as well as for individuals. Persons who hold political power must work within the framework of a just order and commit themselves to the most nonviolent, peaceful solutions possible. And they should work for this within an international order of peace which itself has need of protection and defense against perpetrators of violence. Armament is a mistaken path; disarmament is the commandment of the times. Let no one be deceived: There is no survival for humanity without global peace!

c)   Young people must learn at home and in school that violence may not be a means of settling differences with others. Only thus can a culture of nonviolence be created.

d)   A human person is infinitely precious and must be unconditionally protected. But likewise the lives of animals and plants which inhabit this planet with us deserve protection, preservation, and care. Limitless exploitation of the natural foundations of life, ruthless destruction of the biosphere, and militarization of the cosmos are all outrages. As human beings we have a special responsibility–especially with a view to future generations–for Earth and the cosmos, for the air, water, and soil. We are all intertwined together in this cosmos, and we are all dependent on each other. Each one of us depends on the welfare of all. Therefore, the dominance of humanity over nature and the cosmos must not be encouraged. Instead, we must cultivate living in harmony with nature and the cosmos.

e)   To be authentically human in the spirit of our great religious and ethical traditions means that in public as well as in private life we must be concerned for others and ready to help. We must never be ruthless and brutal. Every people, every race, every religion must show tolerance and respect–indeed high appreciation–for every other. Minorities need protection and support, whether they be racial, ethnic, or religious.

2.   Commitment to a Culture of Solidarity and a Just Economic Order.

Numberless men and women of all regions and religions strive to live their lives in solidarity with one another and to work for authentic fulfillment of their vocations. Nevertheless, all over the world we find endless hunger, deficiency, and need. Not only individuals, but especially unjust institutions and structures are responsible for these tragedies. Millions of people are without work; millions are exploited by poor wages, forced to the edges of society, with their possibilities for the future destroyed. In many lands the gap between the poor and the rich, between the powerful and the powerless is immense. We live in a world in which totalitarian state socialism as well as unbridled capitalism have hollowed out and destroyed many ethical and spiritual values. A materialistic mentality breeds greed for unlimited profit and a grasping for endless plunder. These demands claim more and more of the community's resources without obliging the individual to contribute more. The cancerous social evil of corruption thrives in the developing countries and in the developed countries alike.

a)   In the great ancient religious and ethical traditions of human-kind, we find the directive: *You shall not steal!* Or in positive terms: *Deal honestly and fairly!* Let us reflect anew on the consequences of this ancient directive: No one has the right to rob or dispossess in any way whatsoever any other person or the commonweal. Further, no one has the right to use her or his possessions without concern for the needs of society and Earth.

b)   Where extreme poverty reigns, helplessness and despair spread, and theft occurs again and again for the sake of survival. Where power and wealth are accumulated ruthlessly, feelings of envy, resentment, and deadly hatred and rebellion inevitably well up in the disadvantaged and marginalized. This leads to a vicious circle of violence and counter-vio-lence. Let no one be deceived: There is no global peace without global justice!

c)   Young people must learn at home and in school that property, limited though it may be, carries with it an obligation, and that its uses should at the same time serve the common good. Only thus can a just economic order be built up.

d)   If the plight of the poorest billions of humans on this planet, par-ticularly women and children, is to be improved, the world economy must be structured more justly. Individual good deeds, and assistance projects, indispensable though they be, are insufficient. The participation of all states and the authority of international organizations are needed to build just economic institutions.

A solution which can be supported by all sides must be sought for the debt crisis and the poverty of the dissolving second world, and even more the third world. Of course, conflicts of interest are unavoidable. In the de-veloped countries, a distinction must be made between necessary and lim-itless consumption, between socially beneficial and nonbeneficial uses of property, between justified and unjustified uses of natural resources, and between a profit-only and a socially beneficial and ecologically oriented market economy. Even the developing nations must search their national consciences.

Wherever those ruling threaten to repress those ruled, wherever insti-tutions threaten persons, and wherever might oppresses right, we are ob-ligated to resist–whenever possible nonviolently.

e)   To be authentically human in the spirit of our great religious and ethical traditions means the following:

• We must utilize economic and political power for service to human-ity instead of misusing it in ruthless battles for domination. We must de-velop a spirit of compassion with those who suffer, with special care for the children, the aged, the poor, the disabled, the refugees, and the lonely.

• We must cultivate mutual respect and consideration, so as to reach a reasonable balance of interests, instead of thinking only of unlimited power and unavoidable competitive struggles.

• We must value a sense of moderation and modesty instead of an unquenchable greed for money, prestige, and consumption. In greed humans lose their "souls," their freedom, their composure, their inner peace, and thus that which makes them human.

3. Commitment to a Culture of Tolerance and a Life of Truthfulness.

Numberless women and men of all regions and religions strive to lead lives of honesty and truthfulness. Nevertheless, all over the world we find endless lies and deceit, swindling and hypocrisy, ideology and demagoguery:

• Politicians and business people who use lies as a means to success;

• Mass media which spread ideological propaganda instead of accurate reporting, misinformation instead of information, cynical commercial interest instead of loyalty to the truth;

• Scientists and researchers who give themselves over to morally questionable ideological or political programs or to economic interest groups, or who justify research which violates fundamental ethical values;

• Representatives of religions who dismiss other religions as of little value and who preach fanaticism and intolerance instead of respect and understanding.

a)   In the great ancient religious and ethical traditions of humankind we find the directive: *You shall not lie!* Or in positive terms: *Speak and act truthfully!* Let us reflect anew on the consequences of this ancient directive: No woman or man, no institution, no state or church or religious community has the right to speak lies to other humans.

b)   This is especially true:

• for those who work in the mass media, to whom we entrust the freedom to report for the sake of truth and to whom we thus grant the office of guardian. They do not stand above morality but have the obligation to respect human dignity, human rights, and fundamental values. They are duty-bound to objectivity, fairness, and the preservation of human dignity. They have no right to intrude into individuals' private spheres, to manipulate public opinion, or to distort reality;

• for artists, writers, and scientists, to whom we entrust artistic and academic freedom. They are not exempt from general ethical standards and must serve the truth;

• for the leaders of countries, politicians, and political parties, to whom we entrust our own freedoms. When they lie in the faces of their people, when they manipulate the truth, or when they are guilty of venality or ruthlessness in domestic or foreign affairs, they forsake their credibility and deserve to lose their offices and their voters. Conversely, public opinion should support those politicians who dare to speak the truth to the people at all times;

• finally, for representatives of religion. When they stir up prejudice, hatred, and enmity towards those of different belief, or even incite or legitimize religious wars, they deserve the condemnation of humankind and the loss of their adherents.

Let no one be deceived: There is no global justice without truthfulness and humaneness!

c)   Young people must learn at home and in school to think, speak, and act truthfully. They have a right to information and education to be able to make the decisions that will form their lives. Without an ethical formation they will hardly be able to distinguish the important from the unimportant. In the daily flood of information, ethical standards will help them discern when opinions are portrayed as facts, interests veiled, tendencies exaggerated, and facts twisted.

d)   To be authentically human in the spirit of our great religious and ethical traditions means the following:

• We must not confuse freedom with arbitrariness or pluralism with indifference to truth.

• We must cultivate truthfulness in all our relationships instead of dishonesty, dissembling, and opportunism.

• We must constantly seek truth and incorruptible sincerity instead of spreading ideological or partisan half-truths.

• We must courageously serve the truth and we must remain constant and trustworthy, instead of yielding to opportunistic accommodation to life.

4.   Commitment to a Culture of Equal Rights and Partnership Between Men and Women

Numberless men and women of all regions and religions strive to live their lives in a spirit of partnership and responsible action in the areas of love, sexuality, and family. Nevertheless, all over the world there are condemnable forms of patriarchy, domination of one sex over the other, exploitation of women, sexual misuse of children, and forced prostitution. Too frequently, social inequities force women and even children into prostitution as a means of survival–particularly in less developed countries.

a)   In the great ancient religious and ethical traditions of humankind we find the directive: *You shall not commit sexual immorality!* Or in positive terms: *Respect and love one another!* Let us reflect anew on the consequences of this ancient directive: No one has the right to degrade others to mere sex objects, to lead them into or hold them in sexual dependency.

b)   We condemn sexual exploitation and sexual discrimination as one of the worst forms of human degradation. We have the duty to resist wherever the domination of one sex over the other is preached–even in the name of religious conviction; wherever sexual exploitation is tolerated, wherever prostitution is fostered or children are misused. Let no one be deceived: There is no authentic humaneness without a living together in partnership!

c)   Young people must learn at home and in school that sexuality is not a negative, destructive, or exploitative force, but creative and affirmative. Sexuality as a life-affirming shaper of community can only be effective when partners accept the responsibilities of caring for one another's happiness.

d)   The relationship between women and men should be characterized not by patronizing behavior or exploitation, but by love, partnership, and trustworthiness. Human fulfillment is not identical with sexual pleasure. Sexuality should express and reinforce a loving relationship lived by equal partners.

Some religious traditions know the ideal of a voluntary renunciation of the full use of sexuality. Voluntary renunciation also can be an expression of identity and meaningful fulfillment.

e)   The social institution of marriage, despite all its cultural and religious variety, is characterized by love, loyalty, and permanence. It aims at and should guarantee security and mutual support to husband, wife, and child. It should secure the rights of all family members.

All lands and cultures should develop economic and social relationships which will enable marriage and family life worthy of human beings, especially for older people. Children have a right of access to education. Parents should not exploit children, nor children parents. Their relationships should reflect mutual respect, appreciation, and concern.

f)   To be authentically human in the spirit of our great religious and ethical traditions means the following:

• We need mutual respect, partnership, and understanding, instead of patriarchal domination and degradation, which are expressions of violence and engender counter-violence.

• We need mutual concern, tolerance, readiness for reconciliation, and love, instead of any form of possessive lust or sexual misuse.

Only what has already been experienced in personal and familial relationships can be practiced on the level of nations and religions.

IV. A Transformation of Consciousness!

Historical experience demonstrates the following: Earth cannot be changed for the better unless we achieve a transformation in the consciousness of individuals and in public life. The possibilities for transformation have already been glimpsed in areas such as war and peace, economy, and ecology, where in recent decades fundamental changes have taken place. This transformation must also be achieved in the area of ethics and values!

Every individual has intrinsic dignity and inalienable rights, and each also has an inescapable responsibility for what she or he does and does not do. All our decisions and deeds, even our omissions and failures, have consequences.

Keeping this sense of responsibility alive, deepening it and passing it on to future generations, is the special task of religions.

We are realistic about what we have achieved in this consensus, and so we urge that the following be observed:

1.   A universal consensus on many disputed ethical questions (from bio- and sexual ethics through mass media and scientific ethics to economic and political ethics) will be difficult to attain. Nevertheless, even for many controversial questions, suitable solutions should be attainable in the spirit of the fundamental principles we have jointly developed here.

2.   In many areas of life a new consciousness of ethical responsibility has already arisen. Therefore, we would be pleased if as many professions as possible, such as those of physicians, scientists, business people, journalists, and politicians, would develop up-to-date codes of ethics which would provide specific guidelines for the vexing questions of these particular professions.

3.   Above all, we urge the various communities of faith to formulate their very specific ethics: What does each faith tradition have to say, for example, about the meaning of life and death, the enduring of suffering and the forgiveness of guilt, about selfless sacrifice and the necessity of renunciation, about compassion and joy. These will deepen, and make more specific, the already discernible global ethic.

In conclusion, we appeal to all the inhabitants of this planet. Earth cannot be changed for the better unless the consciousness of individuals is changed. We pledge to work for such transformation in individual and collective consciousness, for the awakening of our spiritual powers through reflection, meditation, prayer, or positive thinking, for a conversion of the heart. Together we can move mountains! Without a willingness to take risks and a readiness to sacrifice there can be no fundamental change in our situation! Therefore, we commit ourselves to a common global ethic, to better mutual understanding, as well as to socially beneficial, peace-fostering, and Earth-friendly ways of life.

We invite all men and women, whether religious or not, to do the same.

Persons Who Signed This Initial Declaration
at the Parliament of the World's Religions

Tan Sri Dato' Seri Ahmad Sarji bin
Abdul-Hamid
Muslim, MALAYSIA

Prof. Masao Abe
Buddhist, JAPAN

Dr. Thelma Adair
Christian, USA

H.R.H. Oseijeman Adefunmi I
Indigenous, USA

Dr. Hamid Ahmed
Muslim, INDIA

Mrs. Mazhar Ahmed
Muslim, INDIA

Pravrajika Amalaprana
Hindu, INDIA

Dastoor Dr. Kersey Antia
Zoroastrian, USA

Mme. Nana Apeadu
Indigenous, GHANA

Dr. M. Aram
Hindu, INDIA

Rev. Wesley Ariarajah
Christian, SWITZERLAND

Dr. A. T. Ariyaratne
Buddhist, SRI LANKA

Imam Dawud Assad
Muslim, USA

Jayashree Athavale-Talwarkar
Hindu, INDIA

H.H. Shri Atmanandji
Jain, INDIA

H.I.G. Bambi Baaba
Indigenous, UGANDA

Rev. Thomas A. Baima
Christian, USA

Dr. Gerald O. Barney
Christian, USA

H.Em. Joseph Cardinal Bernardin
Christian, USA

Mr. Karl Berolzheimer
Jewish, USA

Père Pierre-François de Béthune
Christian, BELGIUM

Dr. Nelvia M. Brady
Christian, USA

Rev. Marcus Braybrooke
Christian, UNITED KINGDOM

Dr. David Breed
Christian, USA

Rabbi Herbert Bronstein
Jewish, USA

Rev. John Buchanan
Christian, USA

Mrs. Radha Burnier
Theosophist, INDIA

Rev. Baroness Cara-Marguerite-Drusilla,
L.P.H.
Neo-Pagan, USA

Mr. Blouke Carus
Christian, USA

Mr. Peter V. Catches
Native American, USA

Sister Joan M. Chatfield, M.M.
Christian, USA

H.H. Swami Chidananda Saraswati
Hindu, INDIA

Swami Chidananda Saraswati Muniji
Hindu, USA

Ms. Juana Conrad
Bahá'í, USA

H.H. The Dalai Lama
Buddhist, INDIA

Swami Dayananda Saraswati
Hindu, USA

Counsellor Jacqueline Delahunt
Bahá'í, USA

Dr. Yvonne Delk
Christian, USA

Sister Pratima Desai
Brahma Kumaris, USA

Dr. Homi Dhalla
Zoroastrian, INDIA

Very Rev. R. Sheldon Duecker
Christian, USA

Prof. Diana L. Eck
Christian, USA

Dr. Wilma Ellis
Bahá'í, USA

Hon. Louis Farrakhan
Muslim, USA

Dr. Leon D. Finney, Jr
Christian, USA

Rev. Dr. James A. Forbes Jr.
Christian, USA

Dr. Rashmikant Gardi
Jain, USA

Mr. Dipchand S. Gardi
Jain, INDIA

Mrs. Maria Svolos Gebhard
Christian, USA

Preah Maha Ghosananda
Buddhist, CAMBODIA

Dr. Daniel Gómez-Ibáñez
Interfaith, USA

Dr. Hamid Abdul Hai
Muslim, USA

Dr. Mohammad Hamidullah
Muslim, UGANDA

B.K. Jagdish Chander Hassija
Brahma Kumaris, INDIA

Rev. Theodore M. Hesburgh, C.S.C.
Christian, USA

Prof. Susannah Heschel
Jewish, USA

Dr. Aziza al - Hibri
Muslim, USA

Mr. Chungliang Al Huang
Taoist, USA

Dr. Asad Husain
Muslim, USA

Dato' Dr. Haji Ismail bin Ibrahim
Muslim, MALAYSIA

Prof. Ephraim Isaac
Jewish, USA

Hon. Narendra P. Jain
Jain, INDIA

Dastoor Dr. Kaikhusroo Minocher
JamaspAsa
Zoroastrian, INDIA

Very Rev. Frederick C. James
Christian, USA

Ma Jaya Bhagavati
Interfaith, USA

Ajahn Phra Maha Surasak Jívānando
Buddhist, USA

Dr. Chatsumarn Kabilsingh
Buddhist, THAILAND

Abbot Timothy Kelly OSB
Christian, USA

Mr. Jim Kenney
Christian, USA

Sadguru Sant Keshavadas
Hindu, INDIA

Siri Singh Sahib Bhai Sahib Harbhajan
Singh Khalsa Yogiji
Sikh, USA

Dr. Irfan Ahmad Khan
Muslim, USA

Dr. Qadir Husain Khan
Muslim, INDIA

Mr. P.V. Krishnayya
Hindu, USA

Dr. Lakshmi Kumari
Hindu, INDIA

Prof. Dr. Hans Küng
Christian, GERMANY

Mr. Peter Laurence
Jewish, USA

Ms. Dolores Leakey
Christian, USA

Rev. Chung Ok Lee
Buddhist, USA

Mrs. Norma U. Levitt
Jewish, USA

Rev. Deborah Ann Light
Neo-Pagan, USA

Mr. Amrish Mahajan
Hindu, USA

Sister Joan Monica McGuire, O.P.
Christian, USA

Imam Warith Deen Mohammed
Muslim, USA

Very Rev. James Parks Morton
Christian, USA

Mr. Archie Mosay
Native American, USA

Dr. Robert Muller
Christian, COSTA RICA

Rev. Albert Nambiaparambil, CMI
Christian, INDIA

Prof. Seyyed Hossein Nasr
Muslim, USA

Prof. James Nelson
Christian, USA

Mr. Charles Nolley
Bahá'í, USA

Rev. Koshin Ogui, Sensei
Buddhist, USA

Dastoor Jehangir Oshidari
Zoroastrian, IRAN

Dr Abdel Rahman Osman
Muslim, USA

Luang Poh Panyananda
Buddhist, THAILAND

Ven. Achahn Dr. Chuen Phangcham
Buddhist, USA

Pravrajika Prabuddhaprana
Hindu, INDIA

B.K. Dadi Prakashmani
Brahma Kumaris, INDIA

Mr. Burton Pretty On Top
Native American, USA

Rev. Dr. David Ramage, Jr.
Christian, USA

Ven. Dr. Havanpola Ratanasara
Buddhist, USA

Dr. Krishna Reddy
Hindu, USA

Prof. V. Madhusudan Reddy
Hindu, INDIA

Mrs. Robert Reneker
Christian, USA

Rev. Dr. Syngman Rhee
Christian, USA

Mr. Rohinton Rivetna
Zoroastrian, USA

Lady Olivia Robertson
Neo-Pagan, EIRE

Most Rev. Placido Rodriguez
Christian, USA

Most Rev. Willy Romélus
Christian, HAITI

Ven. Seung Sahn
Buddhist, USA

Swami Satchidananda
Hindu, USA

Ms. Dorothy Savage
Christian, USA

Rabbi Herman Schaalman
Jewish, USA

Hon. Syed Shahabuddin
Muslim, INDIA

Bhai Mohinder Singh
Sikh, USA

Dr. Karan Singh
Hindu, INDIA

Dr. Mehervan Singh
Sikh, SINGAPORE

Mr. Hardial Singh
Sikh, INDIA

Mr. Indarjit Singh
Sikh, UNITED KINGDOM

Singh Sahib Jathedar Manjit Singh
Sikh, INDIA

Dr. Balwant Singh Hansra
Sikh, USA

H.E. Dr. L. M. Singhvi
Jain, UNITED KINGDOM

Ms. R. Leilani Smith
Bahá'í, USA

Ms. Helen Spector
Jewish, USA

Brother David Steindl-Rast, OSB
Christian, USA

H.H. Satguru Sivaya
Subramuniyaswami
Hindu, USA

Dr. Howard A. Sulkin
Jewish, USA

Ven. Samu Sunim
Buddhist, USA

Hon. Homi Taleyarkhan
Zoroastrian, INDIA

Mr. John B. Taylor
Christian, SWITZERLAND

Brother Wayne Teasdale
Christian, USA

Rev. Margaret Orr Thomas
Christian, USA

Rev. Robert Traer
Unitarian, UNITED KINGDOM

Dr. William F. Vendley
Christian, USA

Pravrajika Vivekaprana
Hindu, INDIA

Prof. Henry Wilson
Christian, SWITZERLAND

Ven. Dr. Mapalagama Wipulasara Maha
Thero
Buddhist, SRI LANKA

Ms. Yael Wurmfeld
Bahá'í, USA

Rev. Addie Wyatt
Christian, USA

H.H. Dr. Bala Siva Yogindra Maharaj
Hindu, INDIA

Baba Metahochi Kofi Zannu
Indigenous, NIGERIA

Dastoor Kobad Zarolia
Zoroastrian, CANADA

Dastoor Mehraban Zarthosty
Zoroastrian, CANADA